"You might as well die here as anywhere"

A Buddhist nun's journey through Zambia

Modgala Louise Duguid

Published by Lulu

"You might as well die here as anywhere"
A Buddhist nun's journey through Zambia
A Lulu book

copyright
© 2011 Modgala Louise Duguid

Published in 2011 by Lulu.com
ISBN: 978-1-4477-0452-2

Book and cover design: Kaspalita

For Amrita

CONTENTS

Acknowledgements — i
Preface — 1
Prologue — 3
1. Unfamiliar Dawn — 5
2. Preparations — 17
3. Learning the ropes — 29
4. Under a southern sky — 45
5. Harsh reality — 61
6. And so to work — 75
7. Friendship — 94
8. On the road — 113
9. Susan's story — 131
10. Adoption — 147
11. The man with no name — 166
12. Christmas in no man's land… — 177
13. In sickness and health — 186
14. Paula's story — 198
15. Joshua's story — 209
16. Stuck in the mud! — 219
17. Mike's story — 237

18.	The Nkoma family	255
19.	Celebration	274
20.	Joy	284
21.	Student days	297
22.	So many goodbyes	316

| About Modgala | 331 |
| About Amida Trust | 332 |

ACKNOWLEDGEMENTS

In writing this book my many friends in Zambia, most named in this book under pseudonyms, walked with me once again. My heartfelt gratitude goes out to them. None of this would have been possible without the support of my teacher Dharmavidya. Thanks also to Prasada and my friends in the Amida Sangha. The loving support of my children Terri and Cameron encouraged me. My family and friends sustained me. Thanks to many for all the practical help, reading of early versions of the book, and encouragement to finally get this book published. Special thanks go to Anna for her proof reading, Padma for advice and sorting my photos and Kaspa for all the technicalities.

Above all I am full of gratitude towards Amrita for her courage in setting up the project, and for her forthrightness and guidance of me in Zambia and beyond.

Love to all – Modgala

www.amidatrust.com   www.amidalondon.org

PREFACE

"You might as well die here as anywhere"

'Here' is Zambia. Joseph looks at me intently as we head towards his village in the bush in the looming twilight. I can see what he's thinking – will I run away as soon as I get sick like my predecessor? I could die here, mosquitoes, snakes and scorpions abound and almost every illness under the sun. His look pierces my heart and I know my/our instinct for someone to come to Zambia as quickly as possible was sound.

How Africa is misunderstood. I know another Africa. A country, Zambia, which is the most peaceful place I have ever lived in. Twelve years ago I lived with the people and was taken into their homes and hearts.

Some years ago my Buddhist group, Amida Trust, had an Activist Training Week. It was during this week that I first met Amrita, a teacher and Primary Health Care Trainer. Lively, excitable, determined, and outspoken, she was dedicated to her vision. She had come looking for help for the Primary Health Care project focusing on AIDS and disabilities that she had started with local Zambians. Together we were ordained and took vows to help all beings.

This book is about the very early days of the project. The story is about Amrita's vision and my journey; above all it is about some wonderful people. For six months I lived with them in the bush villages where there is freedom to move about safely in a society that knows little violence. When I joined Amrita I was fortunate to be embraced by the people and taken into their lives.

It is their story I need to tell, their joy and their suffering: a story about the joy that can be found side by side with suffering when there is friendship. This is the story of my friends.

PROLOGUE

"I want you to go"

It is late September. The Amida community is back in our centre in England. Most of us are at the breakfast table when my teacher Dharmavidya comes in with the news that will change my life. An email has arrived. Mary, who had originally gone back with Amrita to the Zambia project after the summer training in Amida France, to help her establish the project, has been forced to return prematurely because of ill health. My head spins. Amrita is alone again. I know from those late-night conversations in France, around the little shrine in the woods, how hard this new setback must have hit her and the community.

I hear myself say:

"One of us needs to go out as soon as possible".

Silence greets my words; then Dharmavidya looks across the table at me.

"I want you to go"

My response is simple. No hesitation: one word, "Yes"

Very soon the fears start to flood in. I have never travelled on my own before. I have never been beyond our western world. The fears threaten to overwhelm me.

"How can I prepare for what I do not know, or more to the point for what I do know and fear? How will I cope?"

And so my story begins. It is some time now since I returned. I sent extensive letters back; each chapter of this book begins with a quote from my letters. I am not a professional writer, or an intellectual. I am just an ordinary person who had an extra-ordinary experience.

CHAPTER ONE

Unfamiliar Dawn

The captain says it is fine and hot in Lusaka! Now why does that make me think of Star Trek — Ships Log! Maybe I could be called (amongst other things?) a trekkie. Does that go along with being a Buddhist, or am I too irreverent? Faith and irreverence, some combination! I feel the plane losing height. The butterflies in my stomach dance — Breathe - the wheels touch down; slowly the plane taxies in. I have arrived. The heat is palpable as I get out of the aircraft and walk into the building.

Unfamiliar dawn! Woken in the half-light by Naomi's cries I struggle awake.

"Amama ….. Amama ……. AMAMA"

Groans come from other sleepers.

"What's up Naomi?"

Naomi needs desperately to pee so she and her "Amama" struggle over the sleepers out of the room.

Strange noises come from outside the house. As well as the sound of murmuring voices something mechanical breaks the dawn silence, it starts and stops, starts and stops – ohhh, it's the borehole pump, women are drawing water. Where am I? Dimly I make out a doorway into the tiny room we share, there is no door, no curtain even, through it I see a bare white wall, beside my head is my IKEA bag.

More memory surfaces, Lusaka airport, I am the last person in the arrivals section. Only this IKEA bag circles round the baggage reclaim, my rucksack is nowhere to be seen. "No panic," they say – " Just fill in a form!"

"But what about all the medicines?"

I don't say this but I want to. Another passenger had warned me en route that I might have trouble if I declare them. This is a different world. As I plead with the officials to find my bag, I suddenly notice a known face in the doorway. Amrita! I am not expecting her to meet me, am not even sure whether my letters saying that I am coming have reached her. From behind her a tall thin man with a sharply etched face reaches out his hand in welcome, beside her is a beautiful smiling black face. At last I meet Gotami, Amrita's nine-year old adopted daughter, who she has talked so much about. With her is Mike who is the co-founder, and inspiration for, the Tithandizane project. My head clears as I relax in their smiles, even though at the same time I get a telling off from Amrita for coming to the wrong airport – I had found out too late that the airport in Malawi was much closer to Tithandizane.

Amrita and Gotami are lying almost beside me in my new home. A bare footstep separates our mattresses. I lie there, thinking about the long journey in the truck from Lusaka to Tithandizane. On the journey I swiftly became aware of the astounding hospitality of people in Zambia. After a few hours we stopped at a little village where Amrita had left someone en route to Lusaka. She wants to see if he needs a lift, and also feels sure we will be given something to eat. Sure enough the offer is made, and we gladly accept. But first she says, "We must go for a bath."

A bath! How? Where? The small, thatched beehive-shaped huts clustered around a well do not indicate any potential bathroom. We drive a little way out from the village and park the vehicle by the side of the road. I hear the sound of women and children's laughter in the twilight and we follow the voices to find a group bathing in a pool of water. From a distance, deeper men's voices also resound in the sultry air. Shyly I strip off my dusty garments and enter the water to join the joyful group. Hot water! I sit down on the gravelly sand and wash some of the dust out of my hair and relish the feeling of the warm water caressing my body. It doesn't matter that I have no towel or change of clothes. No wonder Amrita was keen to introduce me to this delight! And I, on my first day, have achieved one of my heart's desires. For much of my life I have yearned just to see, let alone bathe in, a hot spring.

Then it is back to the village. In the darkness, rush mats are laid on the ground and I smell food cooking on an open fire. The warm October night surrounds us in velvet blackness. But tired and overwhelmed by this first eventful day, I eat little and just lie down, listening to the soft voices speaking a language new to my ear. I am surprisingly content, free from the fears that preceded my departure. I enter this society knowing I am like a child with all to learn, so I watch and I listen and try to get a feel for this new culture while it nurses me in its arms.

Our long journey continues until finally we reach a cluster of whitewashed buildings close to the road and come to rest beside one of them. I step out of the vehicle tired and dusty and try to take in all the faces that surround me. A dark smiling face approaches, hand outstretched, and a low, deep, slow voice bids me welcome. This is Ndwali, the project manager and full time volunteer. He was a student of Amrita and shared her dream of helping his people deal with AIDS and the other illnesses and disabilities that devastate his country.

Another face bobs into view, another hand, a thin young woman, carrying on her back, tied in a cloth, a tiny child with the biggest eyes I have ever seen, (not that I see them for long as she ducks away behind her "Amama" in fear of this strange woman). I can hardly believe that this slender young woman is Gotami's sister. She is as small as Gotami is large (for her age). They all have a shining beauty. Esther, and her baby Naomi have small well defined features, large eyes, smooth dark skin and close cropped hair, and a very shy manner on this our first meeting. In contrast Gotami has a larger bone structure, broader facial features and long bead decorated hair. When she is happy, she bubbles with exuberance and a huge smile lights up her face.

Crowds of people are waiting for Amrita, so Ndwali takes the chance to introduce me to others at the clinic building nearby. We walk across to the long, low, blue and white building. It is closed for the moment, though a large number of people are gathered in the waiting/meeting area, and on the veranda. I can only smile as I am greeted again and again in a foreign language, Nyanja. However the smiles and handshakes say a lot. I start to learn that this is a country where handshaking is an art. Many different ways to shake hands, many different messages to be found in the handshakes too. I might not understand what is said or exactly what is meant, but by the look of some of the wicked grins, I get the message.

Amidst friendly goodbyes I walk back to our house. Esther is preparing supper in the evening light while Amrita, Gotami and Ndwali have gone to pay their formal respects at a funeral. In Zambia the funeral time is not just that of the final ceremony and burial, but can go on for days allowing all to pay their respects and join the bereaved in their grieving. So I sit on the step and eat the simple supper with Esther and Naomi. As we are eating, some more women and children join us. We start to get to know each other by talking about our families. Fortunately Esther is bilingual, as is the nurse, Margaret, so translations are possible.

"Are you married?"

"I used to be,"

"Oh, is he dead?"

"No, We are separated"

"Don't you miss him? Will you marry again? Do you have children? Don't they miss you?"

Question follows question.

"What church do you belong to?"

This, I will find, is one of the first questions people ask. I hesitate to answer, trying to find words to explain that I am not a Christian.

"I am Buddhist, not Christian".

"Like Amrita?"

"Yes, like Amrita"

"Ah"

It is evident that they are not sure what Buddhism is, but I decide to find out more about their beliefs rather than going into long-winded explanations. I find out that this is a mainly Christian country with many different denominations, all seemingly co-existing harmoniously.

Talking about AIDS is another matter. Margaret mentions the funeral of Amrita's friend and I feel the fear that the subject engenders in the others. I notice their reluctance to face its cruel reality. I can also feel the frustration of the nurse, outspoken in her condemnation of the ignorance that surrounds AIDS.

This has meant the HIV virus has spread, and is still spreading, rapidly.

One woman is quieter than the others. Mrs Nkoma is small and slender. Her cheekbones are very visible, accentuating her lovely smile. She speaks only a little English. Her tiny children do not speak any at all, but make up for it by their exuberant interest in me, even daring to touch me and feel my hair. Its straightness and shine fascinates them. In the months to come, their arms will often surround me as they pull it and plait it. But for now it is the time for us to gradually get to know each other, or rather for them to dare to know this strange white stranger who has come amongst them. Tears come, as I write, remembering those children and their wonderful parents. A letter from Mrs Nkoma sits in my drawer as I write, waiting for an answer. Our friendship is to stretch beyond borders half way across the world.

As darkness falls, the women and children leave. The night is transformed into inky blackness, as Esther, Naomi and I sit on the step. By the soft smoky light of the kerosene lamp I write my first letter back to my other home in England, reassuring all that I have arrived safely. This is the first letter that will constitute the journal of my life in Zambia. I write in it: "It feels good being here – I'm glad I came…"

After some gentle conversation Esther, Naomi and I go to our mattresses. We will not wait up for the others. Sometimes people sit for very long hours at funerals, and who knows what emergencies might encounter them on their way home. I will learn that we always have to get whatever sleep we can, as we never know when a desperate knock at the door might come, and in the majority of mornings we have a very early start. I am tired; this is my first full night's sleep for three days. I sleep soundly, only stirring at the murmuring voices as they return home.

Now fully awake, and musings over, I decide to investigate my surroundings more fully. I sit on the concrete step and take in the different sights and different sounds. Goats career into view – slender goats of many different colours. Chickens peck around in the sandy soil, occasionally jumping up on the step behind me. Ndwali emerges bleary eyed; it had been a late night at the funeral and the sunlight is already blinding. He is hunting for water for washing. Esther reappears, pulling a 20-litre container of water on "shopper" wheels. This I come to realise is a trip that has to be made many times a day. It is amazing how much precious water we need. Every day many backbreaking trips to the borehole are made. However we are lucky, we live right next to it. Many people have to walk a long way to reach a borehole or well and most have no access to a safe water supply. In our travels we can tell by the levels of some illnesses whether the village has a safe and adequate supply of water. Water, I will find, often holds the balance between life and death. The battle against the dehydration caused by many of the illnesses is often won with clean water and ORS (Oral Re-hydration Supplement). We have some special sachets for desperate cases, but soon I learn the correct balance of salt and sugar to put in the precious water to save lives.

I stroll across to the borehole. The women are laughing and giggling as they draw water and this intensifies as I approach. More greetings ensue and they attempt to communicate with me; they have no words of English, and I, as yet, have no words of Nyanja! But, from their gestures, one question becomes clear.

"Can I carry a container of water on my head?"

I shake my head, certainly not one of the twenty litre containers so many women are hefting, or one of the huge iron pots that are used for washing. They give me a little pail, a child size container, and for a few wobbly seconds I balance it on my head.

"No"

I know immediately that I cannot, and will not, ever learn to carry water on my head. I wonder what damage it does to their bodies carrying such heavy loads.

Their giggles increase and they gesture at the lever that works the borehole pump. Surely I can manage that! It looks easy enough. They speed at it, their arms pumping up and down, swiftly filling their containers. At other times their slow leisurely strokes give them plenty of time for laughter and conversation. I watch four hands in unison on the lever as they pump together, enjoying the pleasure of each other's company, and helping each other. I take hold of the lever; I can hardly push it down, and can only manage a weak trickle of water. Then another pair of hands joins mine. I can feel her strength, and seeing the muscles in her thin arms I realise that I am flabby in comparison, even though I had thought myself fit and strong. I am determined to learn, I will practise and develop my muscles too. I vow to become a working part of this community. As their cheerful, friendly laughter sings in my ears I feel their welcome and acceptance.

Later there is a little time for conversation with Amrita. Though we have such different backgrounds, coming from Manchester and London respectively, we are sisters in the Dharma *(Dharma = teachings of the Buddha)*. Our teacher, Dharmavidya gave us our Buddhist names- Amrita and Modgala, in a ceremony affirming our Bodhisattva vows the previous summer. It is the attempted fulfilment of these vows, to help all beings, which has led me to Zambia. As we talk I can feel that the bond with Amrita, which started to form during our Buddhist training, is strong. We have much work to do together.

Meanwhile, as Ndwali starts to educate me in the ways of his world, I realise more fully that I am like a babe in the arms in this complex and initially confusing culture. This day is the start of a learning curve that will never end, both during my stay in Zambia and beyond.

CHAPTER TWO

Preparations

...It was just what I needed to do, no more, no less. No great achievement in that —courage yes, but it comes from a sense of purpose, will, determination to do what I have vowed. I can do nothing less. I feel kind of humble, touched by something...I feel I am, and have been, honed ever since I knew what I must do — have become concentrated, single-pointed, immersed in practice, knowing what is needed. Yet on the other hand humour bubbles up at the very incongruity of this, compared with my old life. Just now I thought, "...what a bleeding palaver!" feeling like Eliza Doolittle in My Fair Lady. "A bleeding guinea pig, that's what I am in this game of life". An experiment, and yet it is serious too. How to be an activist, how to train and be trained? A template for future action, and for a different way of being, practicing, of bringing good to the world. Serious stuff, and yet I have a glorious feel of the humour of it. I laugh, feel warm, and feel OK.

In reality the learning curve had started from the moment I said, "yes" to going to Zambia, and in the next moment started facing my fears.

I had already, in Buddhist terms, "gone forth from the householder life into homelessness," when I left my family home six months previously, to take up the Buddhist life in the Amida Order. I was following the call of the Buddha to help relieve the suffering in the world. Never in my wildest dreams had I expected it to take me to Zambia.

"Yes"

I sit in our shrine room taking in the fears that now confront me, I think about what I do know. I have learnt much about the myriad physical and mental effects of the AIDS virus from youth work and from being a member of a "Buddy Group" in Scotland that supports people living with the AIDS virus. However as I sit this question haunts me,

" How much worse can it be in Zambia?"

I had learnt many details from Amrita. In the area the project covers, there are fifty-eight villages and fifteen thousand people; many show signs of being infected. Until the project started there had been no medical care locally at all. Even now there are few medicines, not even in the distant hospitals, and most people die in their villages because they cannot afford transport to hospital. There is little understanding about the transmission of the AIDS virus, and misperceptions abound. Families care for their sick but are afraid of this new illness and have little idea of how to care for people suffering from its effects. As a Primary Health Care project, a large part of the work lies in finding ways to combat the ignorance, misperceptions, apathy and fear.

I can understand about the fear.

I sit on my meditation stool and face the question that feeds it:

"How on earth can I cope with the conditions?"

Amrita had pulled no punches. For much of the year it is extremely hot, dry and dusty, then when the rain comes, torrential tropical rain, everything turns to mud; mud that carries a myriad of water-borne diseases, mosquito larvae and with the mosquitoes, malaria. Although physically strong I know that I am in some ways a "softy". A Londoner born and bred, I have never adapted very well to country life, despite ten years in the mountains of Scotland. I dread extremes of heat and cold. Also, to a townie, there is scariness about the silence of the country, and the unknown noises that penetrate it. While there is something comfortable about hearing people talk outside your window or front gate, and the soft roar of traffic in the city. The screeching call of an owl or scraping of a tree branch in the middle of the silence of the night is another matter.

The questions spin round as I sit.

"What is the sound of the bush? Will there be hyenas crying in the night, and what do they sound like? Will there be the sound of the drums? What will the people sound like?"

I am sensitive to sounds, easily woken up with the adrenaline flowing and the heart pounding.

"What will it be like to sit on rush mats on dirt floors, fair game for the ants and whatever other strange insects might be found in Africa?"

I have a phobia about insects and for all my life have avoided camping or sleeping rough or in harsh conditions.

"And will I even have a mattress?"

To sleep, eat, and sit on the ground, day after day, month after month feels very daunting! My stomach curls at the thought. I know that Amrita lives with the people and shares their poverty. In the villages few people possess the luxury of a chair, so if one is needed for a special visitor such as a chief or senior official, a neighbour will loan one.

My spirits go up and down in the weeks before my departure, as these fears roll around. I wonder how can I prepare myself?

One answer comes when we are having our regular study of the teachings of the Buddha. In this story about "Fear and Dread" the Buddha talks about how he deliberately went into the forest to confront his fears. Unexpectedly, my teacher, Dharmavidya, turns to me and says,

"Why not follow the Buddha's example?"

I freeze. My mind immediately goes back to the previous summer when I had avoided sleeping in a tent because of my fear of creepy crawlies and the discomfort of sleeping on the hard ground.

"No way," is my swift retort; but then, after a few minutes I wonder what he means.

"What are you suggesting?" I ask hesitantly, in some ways not really wanting to hear the answer.

"If you wish, you could go and sleep alone in a forest."

My mind races ahead. "Sleep in a dark and lonely place full of the sounds of the night? Alone!! Sleep with the earth as my bed, and what would protect me from the elements? No way!"

That response from within me also comes quickly, too quickly. That sheer fact helps me realise that this could be just the right prescription. Buddhist training often means to do that which feels the most difficult! I feel sick with fear at the prospect, and my stomach churns as I contemplate the possibilities.

So one afternoon, a couple of weeks before going to Zambia, I find myself on a rainy day excursion into the Cumbrian hills. As I place my rucksack in the back of the car, I ask myself

"Am I really willing to do this?"

I receive no encouragement from my friends. It has to be my decision alone.

I get out of the car on a hill road in a thick forest in what seems like the middle of nowhere. I walk into the forest as they drive the car away; I don't look back. I am ready to face my demons. Walking deep into the forest, the pine needles lie soft and springy beneath my feet. I search for a suitable spot to put up a sheet of plastic to protect me from the rain. I look at the branches as they sweep down, and at the ground below, hunting for a space with not too many roots to bruise my bones like in the children's fable the *"Princess and the pea"*. Amazing! I actually manage to form a roof over my pine needle bed. I feel triumphant; maybe I am capable of being an explorer after all. I just hope the small piece of plastic will keep out the rain. I curl up in my sleeping bag and despite the October chill I feel quite warm. I lie still and listen to the strange sounds around me. I face my fear.

The demons do not get me, though of course they try. I can hear them! The sounds of the night and the silence try to hypnotise me into my fears. They fail, they do not touch me, I realise there is no brooding presence wanting to get me. It is just night and the sounds I hear are those of small creatures scurrying about their business, and the tree branches singing their songs in the wind. The ants do not eat me alive. I survive! More than that, the fears that had tormented me now come back to a realistic level.

I also have another concern - men! Amrita had joked about how if I were to go to Zambia I would be hotly pursued. Zambians like their women fat! I know that I am not really afraid of the men themselves, I am more concerned about the distraction and sapping of energy it might take to parry their advances, and to keep me out of temptation. Implicit in the vows I have made is the vow of celibacy. There is just too much work to do in the world. I cannot afford the luxury of even thinking about relationships. - Relationships take up much energy, and also, there is the risk that friendliness could be misconstrued by others, if I am not careful.

At the breakfast table I share my concerns with Prasada.

"How can I make my intention clear? How can I keep safe?"

As we talk an idea comes to me: perhaps I could wear an adapted meditation suit. I am surprised at my own suggestion. Since my early, miserable, school days I have hated and rebelled against uniforms. But where can I get one?

Prasada's suggestion is simple and direct,

"Let's buy some cloth and make some."

We go together to a large local store and look for inexpensive durable fabrics in appropriate colours. Bales of cloth of every colour and texture face us. It is fun choosing. However, I have butterflies in my stomach, as the process makes the forthcoming journey start to feel very real! We choose red for my travelling suit, my smart suit, while for day to day wear, working in the hot sun, we decide that cream is more suitable.

Back at the house, on the kitchen table, Prasada cuts a paper pattern from a meditation jacket. It is ideal, fitting comfortably, and simply fastened; to it we add a useful inside pocket. Loose fitting trousers give us a pattern to complete the ensemble. Modest and practical, the suit will protect me against the elements, the rough work, and, we hope, the men!

Julie, one of our local sangha members, makes me three suits. We meet for several fittings, panicking together about getting them finished in time, laughing and crying together. In a way these fittings mark my passage of preparation for this great adventure. The night before I am due to leave, I wear one for the first time, sharing it with our meditation group. I feel strange as I walk down the stairs in it and go to sit on my stool. It is a little tight. I pray the stitching will hold. Excitement wells up from within, I feel the love around me from my community, I grow still inside. The longest journey of my life is close at hand.

Along the way there are many other practical things to do and decisions to be taken, but perhaps the biggest of all is telling, and leaving, my children. I feel sad at leaving them, and being so far away in a country where the postal service is erratic and unreliable, and where there is no way to get to a telephone.

I speak to my daughter Terri.

"Go for it Mum" She says

I am grateful for her encouraging response; at twenty-three she is on the verge of "going for it" herself. Exploring the world that lies beyond studying and university and the confines of this little island called Britain.

My son Cameron is his usual laid back self.

"I knew you would do something like this" is his response.

He has great confidence that his Mum will actually "get out there" and do something. He too is exploring; his is the world of art and music and the friendship of university life. They both come to help me with the packing and send me on my way!

The packing is almost a story in itself. Time and time again my bags are repacked. On and off the scales I struggle. Fat lady with fat rucksack! Every gram counts! The objective is to carry the maximum medicines and minimum personal requisites. Large numbers of medicines, many invaluable pain relief creams and ointments, as well as bandages and painkillers, have been collected from around the country. I just have to get as much to Zambia as possible. Clothes are kept to the absolute minimum, and most are worn on my actual person. I look like a 'teletubby'!

Books are the greatest problem. Books are a lifeline for me; in them I can find inspiration when all seems dark. But they are heavy. Brainwave! I have a waterproof jacket, it is thin, can go over my layers of clothes, and has many copious pockets. Every pocket is filled to capacity. I am now an even a stranger looking '*teletubby*'! The weight of it and its contents are to cause much amusement when I go through customs!

My one piece of hand luggage carries my most precious items. Photos of family and friends; a music tape from my son, Dennis the toy rabbit from my daughter, and a cat card from Dharmavidya's mum Irene, who has become a second mother to me. My birthday gift from Dharmavidya and Prasada comes too, a beautiful little bell with a sweet tone, a miniature of the one we use in Newcastle. To grace my new home I also carry Geske's lovely statue of the Buddha.

The time for departure draws inexorably closer, six months feels a long time to be away from my friends; but with my teacher's guidance, and the love of our community, I find a sense of ever deepening calm. I have faith that I am pursuing the right course, and alongside it arises an intriguing sense of humour and adventure.

CHAPTER THREE

Learning the ropes

...This place and the people do not feel strange to me even though my senses tell me they are — the eye perceives the difference in landscape and the colour of the skins, the ear hears the different language, and the skin feels the dust. And yet the heart feels the same. This land, this earth is the same and we are all people together. I touch joy today — the world is my home.

I start to gather my first impressions of my new home. As I take these in, I realise that it doesn't matter that this is like no other home I have lived in. Many things are a surprise. The biggest one is that the "kitchen" is on the outside rather than the inside. It is a small, open, circular, grass topped shelter, set a little way from the house, close to one of the only two trees anywhere near us. In the "kitchen" three burning logs, separated by stones, heat up a large, scorched, aluminium pan that is balanced rather precariously on top of them. The washing up is also done outside the house, crouching on the sandy soil, using a small plastic bowl with a piece of sacking for a scourer. The crockery is then left to dry in the sun on a tall, rough wooden construction made from thin scrubby branches, high enough to be out of reach of the scavenging goats and chickens.

The "bathroom" too is on the outside, a bit further from the house and beyond the two lonely trees, it is in a dry sandy area waiting to be prepared for growing vegetables when the rainy season arrives. It is a small square brushwood shelter, open to the elements. A few flattish stones enable us to put down the bowl of water when we wash each morning; the stakes supporting the brushwood become our "coat hangers".

The toilet is at a distance from the house, and is a small brick building, built around a very smelly and fly-ridden hole. On the first night I realise how carefully I must put down and pick up my torch, for fear of contacting baby scorpions.

In front of this building lies a dilapidated chicken coop. The brushwood roof has now caved in, and the mud bricks are crumbling away. No wonder the chickens disdain it and are forever trying to get in the house to lay their eggs! A loud crescendo of clucking displays their triumph when they are successful. Not that there is much space for them to hide in, it is not a large house, just a small rectangle of whitewashed mud bricks.

The door into the house opens from a small "veranda" - a narrow stretch of polished concrete. Two small store-rooms, one containing our meagre supply of food and a large clay pot of cool water, the other holding a large drum of diesel for the vehicle. Inside it consists of two small bedrooms off a slightly larger room where much of our business takes place.

The bedroom I am lying in, as I try to get my bearings, is one of these rooms. Here five of us, and all our belongings in our respective bags, squeeze into a room little larger than the average western bathroom. We, three women and two children, share two small single mattresses and a double airbed that keeps deflating. There is one brick shelf high in one corner, stacked with boxes of medicines. A few hooks between the small windows allow us to hang up our day clothes, though from time to time we have to rescue and remove them from the brown line of mud and termites that keeps encroaching on them. On the small windowsill above my bed is my Buddha figure, beside it my bell; while behind them I have arranged pictures of the shrines in France and of my children. Whenever I enter or even look into the room they face me, and at night I curl up beneath them and sleep. Sometimes, I cry with them at seeing all the suffering around me.

Ndwali has the other bedroom, and at present it is his turn to have the only bed. Though he has the room to himself, it is full of bicycles, tools, bags, medicines and anything else of use or value that we jointly possess. His is the room that will leak most badly when the rains come, when the water gets through holes in the corrugated roof that is mostly held on by stones.

Above the communal room, we also have trouble with the roof, and the termites. Some of the beams supporting the corrugated iron have been nearly eaten away. There is real danger that when the winds come it will crash in on us. Some nights we listen to the ominous sounds and pray. More pictures of my children smile down at me from the window ledge high up in this room. There is once again one small white washed brick shelf, high in a corner this time stacked with boxes of condoms. Below it, is a small round table, our only piece of furniture, on which the Buddha, large and white, gazes serenely, surveying us through the lake of papers that surrounds him. Here in this room, we sit and eat on the rush matted floor, meditate, and meet with the streams of people arriving at the door. Often we laugh and let off steam, sometimes rolling around the floor as, at the end of a long day, we sprawl out, easing our aching bodies. This is our home and centre of my life in Zambia.

I arrived ready and willing to do anything, and soon find this means – everything. A knock on our door wakes me at 5.30 on my second morning. Time to get driving. Sand collecting. I ferry truckload after truckload of sand accompanied by young men laughing and joking as they hitch lifts from sand collection pit to the project and back again. Their laughter is infectious, the boys grin and flirt with Gotami, teasing her and throwing comments to each other at the same time as they throw sand into the back of the pick up. They show off their strength and their wit. I feel as if, for the moment, I am back amongst the teenage friends of my son and daughter, or with the youngsters with whom I had worked in Scotland. I might not understand most of the words, but I can interpret the expressions on their faces. Boys showing off seem to be the same everywhere, and Gotami's head tossing and sharp rejoinders perhaps hide some of her shyness.

Between spells of digging the sand the youngsters crawl all over the vehicle fascinated by its inner workings. The ferrying of the sand takes many hours, back and forth time and time again. A stern man, the Induna, or advisor of the village watches us. He is tall and thin, a brooding presence. His face is deeply lined, his eyes are sharp, and he looks at me somewhat suspiciously. I feel rather awkward here, watching, as the boys' dig, not able to help other than by driving them back and forth. But I laugh and smile, and use the time to get to know them, hopefully forming relationships that will prove fruitful in the months to come, as I try to impart information, and provide the condoms that will protect them from the ravages of AIDS.

I also study my surroundings. We are not far from home. I can see the white buildings in the distance, and beyond them low hills that are coloured violet in the heat haze. Between us lie occasional trees and a low flat area of scrubland, as well as a few thatched huts where some of the people live. Around us are a few bushes and trees, struggling to grow in the sandy soil. Where the boys dig, the sand is pure and white. This perfect building sand lies below a layer of thin soil topped by wispy grass.

As the day proceeds the sun grows hotter and progress gets slower. Amrita takes over the driving for a while and I am able to watch another group of villagers at work. They are going back and forth to the hills behind our house gathering stones. The women sway gracefully as they walk surefooted, often without shoes, on the hot sandy ground. They carry large flat round baskets of these stones on their heads bringing them to the men who hammer at them; making small piles of chippings ready to be used for the foundations of the buildings that one day soon they hope, will house the Tithandizane project. It is slow work, but the piles grow steadily.

These first days go by in a blur. Many times I am Ndwali's driver visiting far off villages to remind them about the coming visit of the dentist and eye people, and of the need to collect materials for the promised buildings. Microprojects, an organisation that co-ordinates foreign aid, we hope, will fund and equip the buildings, but only if all natural materials – river sand, building sand and homemade mud bricks are in place first. Then they will inspect the site and decide whether there is enough for the long and complicated process of gaining funding to proceed. Each village has to play its part and time is running out fast. The officials from Microprojects will arrive any day. We also desperately need to get in the river sand before the rains are upon us and the gentle trickles are transformed into raging torrents. Bricks must be brought in from outlying villages before the dirt roads are transformed into rivers of mud, that no lorry can traverse. Many villages have made the mud bricks and somehow these need to be transported ready for the building of the Primary Health Care Centre.

In these journeys I get to know some of the bush roads, and begin to have some idea of the whereabouts of villages. It is confusing, as many villages look similar to my unaccustomed eyes. Most consist of a number of small rectangular straw roofed dwellings, separated by bare sandy soil amidst barren earth fields and shrubby woodland. Some villages are large and sprawling whilst others are compact. Most houses are bare of decoration though occasionally one has a simple painting in earthen colours on its front wall. This barrenness disturbs me; there is a feeling of life and creativity lost. I am experiencing a dawning awareness of the repeated disappointments that these people have suffered, leading to the apathy and lack of hope that seems to envelop this area. The farther from the single tarmac road I travel, the more this becomes apparent. The narrow tracks become progressively more rutted, and bushes scrape the side of the vehicle as we travel.

And yet, there is a beauty in the barrenness, and my senses are stimulated. The sounds of insects hum and chirp in my ears. Birds call out warnings, and sometimes I glimpse a flash of colour in the trees. Leaves on many of the trees feel waxy to the touch, and the smooth sandy soil feels good between my fingers. The sun warms me, and I am surprised to find that this dry heat is nowhere as unpleasant as I had feared.

At each village while Ndwali seeks out the headman, I stand back, demurely waiting to be introduced, to be made known, noticing that usually men and women sit separately. I am not sure of my place and rely on Ndwali indicating what I should do. Most often in these early visits I am treated as an honoured visitor and brought a stool, one of the few each village possesses, to sit near the men as they have their discussion. I sit quietly and listen to the foreign tongue trying to gauge from gestures and expressions how the dialogue is proceeding. This is my role for now, for this moment, not a truck driver/youth worker, but an emissary from afar. Tomorrow it might be different. Most other times, in the months to come, as people know me better, I join the women on the mud steps of their houses or sit with them on the dry dusty earth.

I grow aware of one huge impediment that hinders me. Language. I need to learn at least a smattering – fast. Back at the house on my very first day, I meet my first teacher, Joseph. A man in his early thirties, slim and always smartly dressed, his trousers and shirts pressed to perfection. He, even when squeezed alongside a dozen other people and all their goods into the back of a truck, somehow manages to be free from dust and mud! He is easy to spot from afar when we are out and about in the villages, as he walks with long strides, in his favourite red shirt. He likes to laugh, but is also a serious man, dedicated to improving conditions for his people. He is chairman of the Health Committee and the deputy chairman of Tithandizane, and takes his work seriously.

They are very big on committees in Zambia! He had been instrumental in encouraging those two committees to join forces together to push the local government health board to finally provide a clinic nurse. After a twenty-seven year wait! I guess he is also keen to push me into doing all I can for his community. Joseph starts by teaching me some of the basics of the language, Nyanja, especially greetings and terms to do with health, and sickness. We sit on the floor of our house, and I bring out my little notebook and record the unfamiliar words with unusual spellings, that look and sound so strange and unpronounceable. We laugh as I try to get my tongue round them.

"Molka Bwanji – Good morning"

"Muli bwanji – How are you?"

"Zicomo gombilli – Thank you very much"

Others join us, and laugh even more, especially when I try to pronounce some of the place names:

"Mchala, Nkuti, Mchewa..."

Surnames are even worse:

" Nkoma, Nkanimose, Mnkalamba..."

One of the new arrivals has an especially wicked laugh, and I remember his handshake from the day before. He looks at me and asks:

"Have I learnt the meaning of certain handshakes?"

I smile, "Yes I have learnt, and no, thank you"

He offers me his hand; I put mine behind my back and decline to take his. There is no mistaking the message. Irvine is young and handsome, and knows it. Sex is a major part of life in Zambia. It is much enjoyed - by the men anyway. They are always looking for more, even when they have two wives. It does not feel threatening to me; in this society, a refusal of advances is accepted with a teasing comment and the implication -

"If you change your mind...."

I can see that it is an open and honest appetite; unfortunately it can also lead to contracting AIDS and the other sexual diseases that are rife here. At least Irvine knows the value of condoms and promotes their use vigorously. Sadly many still do not use them, fearing that either they will spoil their enjoyment, or that, because of their strange lubrication, they actually contain the AIDS virus. Much of our work here is about promoting condom use and dispelling of such fallacies as these.

Irvine, like Esther, along with several others is a volunteer CHW (Community Health Worker). They have all done some training to be able to assist people around them. In reality they frequently have to help the nurse at the clinic and are often left in charge. They also go on outreach forays into far-flung villages to help conduct clinics for children under five. Throughout the day Irvine and his fellow workers call into the house, introducing themselves to me, and eating with us. They take great delight in teaching me all they know, and impressing on me the amount of disease and death that is rife in this community. They live, never knowing when death will strike, yet they treat that fact very stoically and interspersed with our serious conversation there is much laughter.

From the little group of CHWs I hear how a number of men and women have been tested recently for AIDS. Out of twenty-one, thirteen had tested positive. They are still reeling from the shock. No official figures have ever indicated that the incidence of infection is so high, and these had all been from just one village. What is even more frightening for them is the total lack of medicines to combat AIDS or the opportunist infections, as well as a general shortage of even the most basic medical necessities. Oh how I hope my bag will turn up! But I keep quiet; not wanting to raise hopes and have them dashed again. Also from them, that very first day I learn much about the country life. The crops, the poor soil, the worry about whether the rains will come, and fear of the portending famine. The food will run out soon, due to the failure of the rains the previous year.

There are many searching questions for me to face. They live their lives openly; they expect me to be the same. I can see them, and will meet their families. They want to know about mine.

"How many children do you have? Where are your parents? Where do you live? Are you married? Do you want a husband? You should have a husband!"

I realise there is no hiding place here, both physically and mentally; and that I am very dependent on others. There is firmness in the way they speak to me.

"You must learn to live here as we do, you must get to know it as it truly is, so you can paint a true picture for your people back in England."

I hear about all their struggles, to get education, food, and health care. I hear about their faith. They are Christians, and seem comfortable in the faith that was introduced by the colonials. There is not much evidence of their old religion at first, however as time goes on I learn more about their beliefs and fears, and about the local healers - the Nyangas. Despite its strangeness to them, because of my lack of belief in a God, they are very acceptant of my religion too.

A few days after my arrival I start to learn a little more about another aspect of their culture. While Ndwali and I had been driving out with messages to far-flung villages, Amrita had gone off on her bicycle. We go to find her. Here I am introduced for the first time to the Ngoma dancing of the Ngoni tribe. And here she is, dancing along with them. It is an amazing sight. A circle of men holding spears, chanting, and turning, this way and that, swirling, shouting and stamping, their animal skins flying, Amrita is one of the team, one of few women who join in the dance; she looks the part and her presence is welcomed by all.

Amrita got one of the local tailors to make her outfit from fake animal skins, very important for her, because one of her main concerns in life is to try and save animals from suffering. A circle of women surrounds the dancers, calling and encouraging. Men loll further back against the walls of the huts watching and assessing. One or two more important men sit in chairs. I am given a chair at one point, and feel very uncomfortable so I stand up and join in, feeling much happier amongst the women who circle the dancers, clapping and cheering them on, their whoops adding to the spectacle.

Above all, these first days involve getting to know the young. Children everywhere flock to the vehicle calling out for Amrita. They are surprised to see this very different white face! Later that evening, back at the house, another treat awaits me. The local village children have come to dance for me, forming a belated welcome party. Their smaller bodies mimic some of the actions I had seen in the dancing earlier. Their enthusiasm is infectious and I feel drawn to join in. I love to dance, but sudden shyness and wariness holds me back. The drums are calling me, I feel the rhythm, the sensuousness of the life within the dry, dusty, often aridly beautiful arena. I go back into our house happy and join the others sprawling on the floor, ignoring the scorpions and the ants, and we find some precious time to talk, and laugh and get to know each other better.

CHAPTER FOUR

Under a Southern Sky

I contemplate the moon. It is full, and hung, huge and yellow against the inky black sky and a different horizon to one I have ever known. A different sky, a Southern sky, still somewhat alien to me as I see the different configurations of stars, but I know even so, that it is the same sky. I think of home.

I start to get to know my new family as we live and work together. Amrita's tough exterior shelters a soft heart. Often all that can be seen is her fierce determination to get things done. To make the people do something, anything, to get out of the apathetic rut they have slipped into, villagers and officials alike. I am amazed by the work she has done, forming plans, meeting officials, seeking out help in order to get the project off the ground. She is inundated with pleas for help, for advice on health care issues. She is a driving force behind Tithandizane. I see her get angry at the apathy and neglect but often I see her hurting deeply as she sees her friends suffer, and all too often, die. I grow to love her and sometimes to hate her as we live and work like sisters together. I see her love for her adopted daughter Gotami, a fierce motherly love that sometimes explodes with frustration.

Gotami of the huge smile can also get very downhearted and defiant. Because of her large size, she looks much older than nine. She also looks different, with her long hair swinging with multi-coloured beads. She comes in for a lot of teasing from the other children. She is bright beyond her years too. When she bothers to write she speaks with a voice of clarity and wisdom. But she hates school! So there are battles. She is much happier taking care of the little library and reading all the books - or playing of course!

I reckon Esther is bright too, but she, in her twenty years, has not benefited from much education, and now she is too engrossed in being cook and caretaker of this extended family. It is often a thankless task for her, fetching water, making fires, cooking, washing, sweeping, all the while being tormented by her little scamp of a daughter Naomi, who tiny as she is will ball up her fists and stand up to very much bigger children, and her mother.

From Esther I learn much about the difficulties of a woman growing up into a patriarchal society. She belongs to a matrilineal tribe from another area and shares her observations of the women in the local area. They are mostly of the Ngoni tribe and grow up learning to curtsey to the men; to see to the men's needs first, to entertain them, especially sexually, and in the men's presence, much of the time to keep silent. I learn a little more about women's rituals and the dancing they are taught to entertain and keep their men. Dances taught as they enter puberty and their menstrual cycles begin. Dances too to enhance the men's pleasure in the sexual act. Though the way they are described gives me the suspicion that they add to the women's pleasure too. When women get together laughter resounds, and their real characters shine through.

I start to get the feel of a woman's life as, in a small way, I help Esther wash and clean. I can see the artistry in her patterns that she sweeps in the sand that surrounds the house. I can feel her care as she attempts to cook the best meal she is able to out of the frugal ingredients. And I appreciate the sheer hard work she puts in; as she answers queries, finds things that we need, and dresses wounds. She is in a way another daughter for me, but more than that is my teacher in the way of womanhood in Zambia.

I know that because of the melting pot of tribes in Zambia, that this is a very particular glimpse. It is also a glimpse of life out in the bush, where old ways still remain. Life is quite different in the towns. In the bush, the pleas that the government are making for women to achieve more equal rights, and to take charge of their health, are only just being heard and taken notice of. On the other hand the old customs and sense of respect they engender are perhaps, what give rise to the peace and safety I also find in the bush.

I gradually start to come to know Ndwali. He is complex in some ways; in part a product of his patriarchal ancestry, and in part a modern, more enlightened man. He is not a man of many words. In some ways he can seem slow and uninterested, but I came to realise that he is weighing up the situation to try to steer the wisest course. Sometimes though, he can be just avoiding things. He often deflects much tension by his sometimes-outrageous sense of humour, though it can get him into trouble too! This humour however hides a deep seriousness and care for his community, and sometimes through it I can see the pain he suffers at the conditions people have to endure. People come looking for him at all hours, especially the young. He rarely has a bad word to say for anyone. My respect for him grows. His slowness of action is a good foil for Amrita's quickness. They are a good team.

In these early days and weeks, I also try to get to know the wider community that I have joined. I struggle to read, understand and pronounce the local place names, which to me sound very complex, starting with odd-looking combinations of consonants: Ng, Mch, Mk and so on. The main tribes in this area are the Ngoni and the Chewa. They have somewhat different customs; the Ngoni are patrilineal and here the men are bowed to and take control of almost everything, while the Chewa are matrilineal and the women have a bigger say in their own affairs; especially because they stay in their own village after marriage. They have somewhat different dialects too. All this is very confusing for a newcomer. I definitely learn in Zambia to keep hold of my *"beginners' mind"*. Shunryu Suzuki, a master of the Zen tradition of Buddhism in particular exhorts us to maintain this openness, not clinging to what is known but being open to what each encounter brings.

We search for a local map of the villages to help my understanding and help orientate my travelling both walking and driving. We know there are supposed to be fifty-eight villages, but when Amrita draws up a comprehensive map we find the numbers have grown to sixty-three. Other villages round the edges of the area have crept in to make use of the growing facilities.

Amrita and Ndwali show me the plans for Tithandizane. Different buildings will eventually be built to accommodate people according to their different needs. Badly needed is a short-stay ward where families can learn how to care for people with AIDS. Also needed are a community hall and a house to accommodate the workers as well as workshops for the disabled, the HIV+ and the youth where they can learn skills.

A mother and baby unit would also be useful to offer space to teach mothers with badly malnourished children how to cook soya and other nourishing foods. Then they will go back to their villages and teach others. For a while, earlier in the year when soya porridge powder had been donated, Esther had been teaching some soya cookery to improve the weights of underweight toddlers. The customary removal of the husks from the maize when grinding does not help their already limited nutrition. Unfortunately much of its nutritional value is lost through the removal. The sound of pounding is a regular heartbeat in the villages as the women seek to whiten the flour. Our own eating of mugywa, un-pounded maize, sets a good example. It tastes much better too; when eating with others out on the road I struggle to eat the cooked pounded mealie meal.

Education is the main thrust of Primary Health Care, empowering people to take care of their own health and lives. It is impeded by illiteracy and lack of opportunity to gain an education. Unfortunately education in general is becoming harder to obtain for the people here. There is a shortage of educational materials, and parents struggle to find the small fees even a basic education entails. Many bright young men and women come to me asking where they can find help. Basic education often carries on for many years often due to a pregnancy. This is why Esther at twenty is doing her exams. I study geography with her for a couple of days. Through this I learn much more about this beautiful and sadly mistreated country. In this area, like many, the already poor soil has been further depleted by the growing of food crops such as maize, whose hybrid seeds supposed to give high yields, are not native to the country, They are grown in the same fields year after year and need a large amount of costly artificial fertilisers, as do cash crops like cotton and tobacco.

Esther is due to leave us for a couple of weeks to take these examinations. Time for me to get domesticated! With so little furniture there is no need for much housework, but it is a constant battle against the dust and the chickens and the termites. Red trails lead down the white washed walls where they make their forays. I also need to learn to cook – village style. This is done on a wood fire or, when the rains come, on one small charcoal brazier. A meal is cooked in two pots to be eaten sometime in the early afternoon. Timing depends on when families return from the fields.

We share the poverty of the villagers. Even in normal times there is only one main meal each day, and that consists of nchima, a kind of mealie meal dumpling served with a little bit of sauce called relish, to go with it. Occasionally we might have some porridge for breakfast or for supper some sweet maize fritters. Otherwise we just have plain bread buns; as an occasional treat we have a little margarine. If we are lucky, we might have some groundnuts dry roasted in a pan on the brazier, or, very occasionally some of the best peanut butter I have ever tasted. Thanks to Esther's sheer hard work, as she has pounded it in a pestle and mortar. But I am afraid I will never become a very proficient cook. I am much better at washing up, and as time goes on, fetching water.

Nchima, is the staple food. Ground maize meal is made into a stiff porridge. There is an art to stirring the mealie meal into the boiling water, then, when it is cooked into porridge, a second lot of meal is added. It takes strong muscles to stir this mixture. I never become very adept at making it. I make a very sad-looking attempt at forming it into the neat ovals that are usually piled onto the plate.

Very occasionally we have rice. I can cook that, and can make a reasonable relish of curried vegetables to go with it. Sometimes it is cabbage, fried with a little tomato and onions, another time beans. When the mushrooms come up, along with the rains, they are practically all we have to eat for weeks on end. When the pumpkins start to grow leaves, these leaves, with their veins carefully skinned off, make a tasty relish. Though we have to be careful how many we take from each plant. Cowpeas leaves are good too, especially the ones from the previous year, which have been dried and stored in round balls of larger leaves. A big treat is a few potatoes diced into a curry sauce.

Life is very frugal at the best of times, but in the months before the harvest there are days without much of a meal as we share what we have with visitors. Sometimes Esther goes to the cupboard and finds it bare our meagre stocks given away. One time, after a long day out in the bush, all the food was gone and all I could find in the cupboard was rotting mangoes. I still cannot look a mango in the eye today, let alone eat one, my stomach turns as I remember. We seemed to live on mangoes for weeks on end; they were all people had to give and we could not refuse them! People are glad to give something, anything to help us keep going. Just before I leave the first crops are being harvested, and there is great joy for many people as they introduce me to new delicacies. Fresh maize cobs, lightly boiled in salted water, or burnt black when roasted on hot coals. Dark green pumpkins, whose tough skin hides a dense, sweet, yet floury, orange flesh. Groundnuts, that are eaten freshly picked or, strangely, boiled before shelling, make an unusual stomach filler.

Eating is a ritual: we sit in a circle, our legs pointing outwards. A bowl of water for washing our hands is held out to the visitors first and then passed on round the circle, each of us holding it for the next person to use, the children going last. A plastic jug, full of cool water taken from the giant clay pot that sits in a shady corner of the small store, fills our battered plastic cups. Then we pass around the food, each of us taking some nchima and a little relish onto our small, sand-scraped tin or plastic plates. We make the nchima into little round balls that we dip into the relish. This is a mucky job, especially for a beginner! I am glad that afterwards the bowl of hand washing water is passed round again. At public events this is done outside, each person pouring the water over another's hands. Though, in fact, the origin of this is practical because of the fear of cholera, I find this a most lovely ritual, drawing me closer to the people who enable me to wash my hands and to those to whom I am able to offer this little service.

The communal meals, which are shared with anyone visiting, are a source of joy for me, much allaying the discomfort of sitting on the floor. In fact on my return to Newcastle, I have great difficulty re-adapting to chairs!

In another house nearby, we do sit in chairs; it is a complete change of scene. This is a large white sprawling house the front steps and veranda are bordered by bushes, that once the rains come, are covered in bright pink flowers. There is ample room to park on the concrete frontage. At the side of the house is a swing chair, and near the side entrance is another small building. This building is dark and squat; it houses the wood stoves that the MP's wives and employees use to do the cooking, despite the fact that a bright and airy kitchen lies within the main house.

Inside it looks like any western house, clean white walls, comfortable furniture, a large dining table and chairs, even a television. There are bedrooms with proper beds, and bathrooms and toilets with running water. It feels a little surreal after days spent in the mud brick huts of the villages and nights in our little, crowded, white house.

The noise of a generator permeates the evening for a distance around this house. We visit frequently because we are kindly allowed to plug in Tithandizane's computer to write letters, to make plans, and to do the accounts. However we also go just to visit the family. We are made very welcome by the MP, and by both of his wives. Their kindness and generosity comforts and soothes us many times. They become good friends to me during my stay there. In the time of hunger, they also struggle, yet always when we visit they find something for us to eat, even cooking it specially. The house is beautiful, and needs much work to keep it clean, with all the children and visitors and constant dust. I come to admire them very much. The life of an MP's wife in Zambia is not an easy one. They do have some people working for them, but always the wives are working, in the house, in the kitchen, and in the fields.

Most of the time the MP's house seems full of children and young people; they range from five years old to late twenties. I spend my first Christmas ever away from my children in Zambia. I miss them very much. Miss the conversations and laughter they bring with them. But here in the MP's house I have adopted another family, or rather they have adopted me! They call me "Ambuya," "grandmother." I am honoured by the affectionate title; but a little bemused. Changing role from Mother to Grandmother within months! I spend Christmas Eve baking with them, teaching them new recipes and having fun tasting all the different mixtures. It is nice to be able to do something in return for all the kindness shown by the family. It feels surreal though, baking in the sweltering heat instead of the snow and ice of Scotland. And cooking on the wood fired stove in their outhouse kitchen.

On my first visit however, there are some strong words for me from the junior wife. Mary, my predecessor had only been able to stay a month because she became sick. Mrs T is still hurting from her rapid departure and the loss of the friendship they had built up. She is also concerned about the effect of the rapid departure on the people. In no uncertain terms she warns me not to do the same.

"It would destroy the faith and trust here, I doubt they would be able to welcome another if you were to do the same"; she cautions.

Amrita's vision has brought great hopes to an area that has been sunk into a deep apathy born out of long-term neglect. In the previous thirty years life had taken a downhill turn as high inflation, a drop in value of copper, their main export, and crippling interest rates had left little in the country's coffers for maintaining, health services, education, and public services. It felt like Zambia had been forgotten by the world.

Mrs T's next words:

"I hope you will stay for life! Maybe we should find you a Zambian husband."

Thrill and daunt me.

I go back to our little house quite shaken by this conversation, I know I have to stick things out "come hell or high water". I know that I must not leave before the end of my proposed stay, unless I am desperately sick. The sense of responsibility threatens to overwhelm me. I lay in my bed wanting to cry. I feel so alone, and in a strange way, undefended. I go out to sit on a log outside. Too much is being asked of me,

"What can I do?"

I feel I know nothing, am nothing, when I look at the people here. See their courage, their integrity, their friendliness, and their generosity - all in the face of unimaginable suffering. I feel deeply humbled by my reception into this community. What I am coming to realise, and the conversation with Mrs T has highlighted it, is that they not only want concrete help, but also they want their plight to be heard and witnessed. I vow to be a witness, and tell their story, that is the least I can do.

CHAPTER FIVE

Harsh Reality

The burial today was poignant, so silent, as if he had been still born – not an adult's or a child's funeral. A little grave for a little body, lined with leaves, covered with a mound of earth, and protected with branches.

It is nearly midnight. There is a knock on the door. There comes a desperate plea. The nurse is away, a young mother to be, pregnant with her first child, has been in labour for a very long time, labour has gone on much too long, can we help? She lives in a village not far away, but a long way from any hospital or from another clinic. She is with her mother and a traditional birth attendant. Birth attendants have some training to assist at simple births, but do not usually attend first pregnancies, as they are the responsibility of the clinic staff. She has been booked to go into hospital, but labour has started several weeks early.

We get in the vehicle and go to see her, prepared to take her on to the next clinic for delivery as, unfortunately, the local nurse refuses to attend her. I go with Amrita because she has not had children. I have experienced giving birth three times but have never been there for another's, so I go there with some anxiety wondering what we will encounter.

We go into the little house. It is very dark; I can see the shapes of a few women around the mum to be who is sitting in the middle of the floor. She is sweating and moaning, obviously frightened and distressed. I follow Amrita in and put my hand on the young woman's shoulder, partly to try to help calm her, and partly to feel the rhythm of the contractions. I look up at Amrita and ask her to find out how long she has been in labour.

"Nearly twenty-four hours"

This is a frighteningly long time. I recall my own long labours safely in hospital receiving much needed medical assistance. What else do we need to know? Ah, yes: "How often is she having contractions?"

"Every couple of minutes."

Birth could be soon, less than every couple of minutes she clutches her abdomen and moans and then lies back against her mother exhausted. It has gone on too long perhaps. There is a desperate need for more expert help.

We help her out to the vehicle, pausing while she bends over as another contraction tautens her body. With an effort she heaves herself up the high step onto the back seat, her mother gets in beside her, while I walk round to the other side and also get in. Together her mother and I support her and try to comfort her. We set off, hoping to find a nurse at the next clinic, nearly thirty kilometres away. If there is no one there then at least we are en route to the hospital.

I look at her as we go along; she looks so young; she is little more than a child. I can feel her narrow thin shoulders beneath my arm.

I learn that in this culture it is acceptable for girls to have a baby very young to prove to potential husbands that they are fertile. There is no stigma attached to being an unmarried mother, quite the opposite. Though the father of the child does have to pay "damages" and the child often goes on to live with grandparents if the mother marries a different man to the father. Having a baby is a source of pride, and they are much loved. Most women of childbearing age seem to have a baby slung on their breast or back, wrapped up in a colourful cloth, the all purpose chitengi. This is a rectangle of brightly patterned material that can also double as a shawl, skirt, sheet, or towel.

The journey seems to be taking forever. The contractions are strong and close together, and birth is imminent. The young woman is frightened, in pain and exhausted. All I can do is hold her and soothe her. Keep her calm – I whisper: "Breathe – breathe".

I pray that the baby will hold on just a little while longer, and that the mother will hold on to her consciousness to help push baby out when the time comes.

We make it to the clinic; fortunately the nurse is here at this one, and it is much better equipped than our one. There are a couple of tables with boxes and instruments, some decent lighting, and a proper delivery table. The young woman walks slowly in with us, then lies down on the table. Within minutes the baby is born; at the end of the day he slips easily out from between her legs.

This is the first birth I have ever watched; it is a very different experience being present while another gives birth, to being the one on the delivery table. It is almost more miraculous in a way, as I witness the wonder of a new life coming into the world. With my first two babies I had been so exhausted and drugged up that I was not fully conscious after very long labours. With my last child I had been full of fear that something might be wrong with him, as there had been with my son Stuart, who died at a few months old.

As I look at this newborn baby, I also feel fearful. He is very tiny, and not quite perfectly formed, something is wrong with the formation of his ears. More worryingly, he does not cry. Suction tubes are applied at first, to no avail; he is held up by his tiny feet and his bottom smacked again and again, eventually a thin cry indicating that he has at least some will to live. He is swaddled up and we leave him and his tired but proud young Mum to sleep at the clinic, while we return his grandmother to her home village. We can only hope that he will survive.

Amrita and I talk as we drive back to our house. I find out more about the perils of home deliveries. Many babies die at birth, mothers too, often because when things get difficult they do not manage to get to the hospital. Many more children die in their first few years of life.

I found out more from the nurse one day when I helped her with the mother and baby clinic. I could see from the pregnant mums' record cards how many failed pregnancies they had had. Margaret gets angry with the mothers for not coming more regularly for their antenatal clinics, to keep a check on their pregnancies, and despairs when they do not bring their babies and toddlers for check-ups and vaccinations. Antenatal check-ups are vital out here in the bush, signs that might indicate a problematic labour are watched for, so that a hospital delivery can be arranged. The problem is the difficulty and expense of getting to hospital and back home again; it is off-putting to parents and sometimes it is impossible for them to raise funds, so many take a risk and have a home birth anyway.

One big problem at home births is the frequent use of dirty threads, often torn from the chitengis, that are used to tie off the umbilical cord, rather than buying and using a sterile thread. A high risk of infection, and worst of all, tetanus ensues.

I will never forget the drawn and agonised face of a one-week old baby I saw with tetanus.

Early one morning there is a knock on the door of our house. Two women stand there with a tiny baby wrapped up in a shawl. She holds up the child for me to see.

"Please help," she says.

I can see how sick he is; his wizened face is grey and old looking. I take them over to the nurse's house and try to wake her up. Sleepily she opens the door, then looks at the infant and shakes her head.

"I can do nothing this baby needs the hospital"

She tells them to get on the road now, and hitch a lift to hospital; it is the only chance. I cannot help; Amrita is already away with the vehicle. I can only join the nurse in her pleas. We both can see the mother's reluctance to go to hospital. We try hard to convince her, but sadly we watch them walk away, back into the bush, taking the baby home to die.

If a baby survives the crucial weeks after birth he is then prey to other diseases. Measles and whooping cough are killers and polio still lurks. The most vulnerable time is between eighteen months and two years, when they are weaned due to the mother's latest pregnancy, or soon after the new one is born. At the clinic the mothers are routinely given chloroquine, as are babies with any sign of a fever because malaria is a major killer of under-fives; together with malnutrition and all the water-borne diseases, it is no wonder that so few babies survive.

I am learning here that less than half the children born make it to adulthood. I fear that the numbers "making it" will reduce even further. I am starting to see many desperately thin and weakly older babies; "AIDS" babies born to unknowingly infected mothers. Often their open mouths revealed a thick white coating; this is candida or "thrush", as it is known colloquially. It is a fungal infection frequently found in young babies and their mothers. However it is also one of the many opportunist infections that haunt people with the AIDS virus. Seeing it in the mouth can indicate that it is overtaking other organs of the body. In people with AIDS, Amrita believes, it is the major cause of the immune system breaking down and consequently a major cause of death here in Zambia, though in the Western world it is controllable by drugs.

These drugs are practically unavailable in Zambia as the price of them is beyond the fragile economy. In a report in 2001 Larry Elliot in the Guardian wrote about the Zambian economy: *"Its plight is summed up in one statistic: the country needs to spend $25 for each person annually on healthcare; it is actually spending less than $3."*

I am seeing the reality behind the bare statistics.

There is also a high risk to women in pregnancy. One day Ndwali announced that we had a very sad job to do. We have a body to collect from a hospital mortuary; a young woman, who had died yesterday just a week after having a miscarriage. We set out for the hospital mortuary, carrying a group of patients for the hospital with us, we try never to travel with a less than full vehicle. It is a long journey to the hospital, more than an hour on a road full of potholes.

We take the patients to the front of the hospital. It is just like many old fashioned small hospitals. It consists of a scattered collection of buildings; some linked with walkways, some single story, while others have several floors. Grey or drably white washed walls give no hint of welcome from the outside. A few trees are scattered round the edges. On the inside there is also much greyness in the wards, though some blue in the corridors gives a touch of colour. Prefab buildings nearby house various offices and outpatient clinics. I will come to know them very well, especially the building housing the tuberculosis clinic. In the main hospital I will get to know the general wards and in particular the maternity ward. Sadly this visit is not to maternity, where the young mother-to-be had been taken a week previously, but to the mortuary.

We return to the main gate of the hospital and go round back lanes to a side entrance to find the mortuary, to the place where the bodies can be collected. In front of the mortuary stands a large solitary tree. Under the tree is a truck with a couple of waiting men, members of a grieving family. Near the door to the mortuary stands another group, just waiting, the women sobbing and the men with stony faces. The grey door is open and through it I can see a walkway, to the left of which is a simple low building where many more people are waiting, standing and sitting on the concrete floor. As also I wait, now and again, I hear the strains of a hymn echoing through the entrance. Opposite this waiting area a door leads into the mortuary itself. From time to time I see small groups of women relatives entering to prepare the body of their loved ones

The group waiting for us to arrive stands outside the mortuary entrance. The body of the young woman is ready for the journey to her final resting place; we just have to wait for the paper work. I look at the woman who is crying and wailing bitterly as she waits. She must be about my age. I learn that her daughter was the same age as mine. Ndwali goes to speak to her, they talk softly and then Ndwali and some of the men go in through the doorway. I sit in the vehicle, close to that doorway waiting. I have nothing I can say; I feel tears in me as I see the mother cry, hear her soft wailing, then hear the wailing increase in volume as the coffin is carried into view.

I hear some rattles and a thump as Ndwali lets down the back flap of the pick-up. I hear a rumble and feel the vehicle shudder as the coffin is lowered onto the bare metal floor. I dare not look; I lower my eyes and let the tears roll down my cheeks. I look at her mother as she comes into the vehicle to sit behind me. We exchange something I cannot really explain… An understanding of the pain that comes from loving and losing our children; a knowing that is beyond time.

Soft thumps follow as people get into the back and sit round the coffin, then the hymn singing commences and the sad sweet tones accompany us on the slow drive back to her home village. Her mother sits behind me, crying all the way. Death may be commonplace in Zambia, but the suffering and grief is the same no matter where one lives.

This is the first of many such slow drives I am to make. Bringing a body back from hospital often leaves a family in debt for many years. Very often because of this fear, the sick are not taken to hospital, and die in their villages, or even more sadly go to the hospital too late for anything to be done. The truck that has been donated to us is a godsend. If we take people to hospital, we are honour-bound to bring them home, one way or another. We are also prevailed upon time after time to bring bodies back for families who would otherwise be crippled by debt. As time goes on the numbers of people presenting themselves for transport to hospital increase until we have to reserve space for only the most desperately needy.

More sad news comes one late afternoon. We hear that the baby I helped deliver has died. He had been too premature, deaf, and the deformed ears possibly indicated other troubles. I am working by our house about midday when the word comes. We do not know when the burial will take place; we just have to wait and watch, as it will take place not far from us. A little later Esther notices a procession picking their way through the bush. Ndwali and Amrita are working elsewhere. Esther has to stay with Naomi, as children are not allowed at funerals, so I walk alone, between the nearby houses, through the fields waiting for rain and out into the bush to join the file of women silently heading towards the hills.

I make my way towards them and see how reverently they are carrying the little bundle. I am touched deeply on seeing it. My son Stuart had been cremated in a tiny white coffin. At his funeral it was the size of the coffin, and seeing it disappear downward on its plinth to meet the flames, that had finally taken me out of all the crazy feelings into the beginnings of an acceptance that he was dead.

His death had come out of the blue. I found Stuart dead in his carrycot beside our bed when he was three and a half months old. I had had no warning. One night I put him to bed, he looked fine apart from a few sniffles. The next morning he was dead. Quickly and silently, in the middle of the night a virus had overwhelmed his lungs.

This baby has no coffin. He is bound in a simple cloth and carried in the arms of his mother. I walk with the group of silent women. No hymns accompany this funeral. No wails of protest sound. This is silent grief as if this child had never lived, had been stillborn, never to see the light of day.

There is a strange solemnity as these women lay their tiny bundle in the ready dug grave amongst the trees. Lay him as if to rest, in a bed of leaves. They stand back, still and silent. The women sit and watch from amongst the trees, witnessing. I join them in their silence; I see silent tears flowing down many faces; I feel them slide down mine. I am grieving too, remembering and sharing in the sorrow of the women…

The mother puts the first spade-full of earth over the tiny body, then one by one other women get up to take their turn. The mound of earth above him grows, over the tiny grave, branches are lain to deter marauding animals. Such a simple ritual, and yet in this shaded woodland graveside there is some beauty in our suffering sisterhood.

CHAPTER SIX

And so to work

It is pandemonium! A social occasion in fact as families and friends meet up. Esther barely emerged from the kitchen as more and more joined us for our snatched meal later in the afternoon; in fact, she had to cook several meals.

The big day arrives. People start arriving soon after dawn. The murmur of their voices wakes us, and Amrita leaps into action immediately, throwing on her clothes and getting into the vehicle and away before we hardly have time to realise what is happening. She has set off to some of the furthest flung villages to collect people. This is the first time ever that a dentist has come to the area. This is also the much-awaited return visit of the optician.

Until Amrita and Ndwali helped set up Tithandizane, which is a Zambian society, and is dedicated to Primary Health Care, earlier in the year no optical or dental assistance was available at all in this area. That is why even this early in the day, just as dawn is breaking, there are already considerable queues.

The mothers are coming too, bringing their small children to the antenatal clinic for check-ups and inoculation. There are large queues outside the nurse's room and she has not yet arrived. When Amrita returns with yet another truckload of people, it is my turn to collect the people with eye problems from the villages. Meanwhile Amrita and Ndwali are called on for all sorts of advice, shuttling back and forth between the Tithandizane room at the clinic and the house.

Sheer chaos. It is time to start making up the lists. The elderly, who are being checked for operable cataracts, are our first priority, as well as those who had the operation last time round and are due for a check up. I am detailed to help Ndwali with this, while Amrita assists the dentist. For me it is a nightmare of unpronounceable and un-spellable names.

I nervously approach the first elderly man sitting on the blue painted bench in the waiting room. I wave my piece of white paper and smile:

"Name?"

I receive a blank look

"Zena?"

I tentatively try to get my tongue round this new word "Eh?"

"Ze…na?"

"Ah Nd…"

Oh…I make an apologetic face, shaking my head, and thrust the paper in front of him, trying to indicate that he should write it for me. Fortunately someone nearby cottons on to my struggle, and in rapid Nyanja explains my predicament. The old man looks at me and laughs; there are ripples of laughter round me. He pulls out a tattered grey card, and points out his name. I try to get my tongue round it. More laughter! Nice laughter, friendly laughter. I am a good source of laughter that morning in the optician's waiting room. Most people then bring out cards to help this funny woman who cannot speak their language.

But it gets worse. Next I have to call out the names for them to go into another room to see the optician. Each time I have to make several repetitions before the person I am calling realises that it is his or her name I am mispronouncing.

It is not just a few that I have to call, either. The waiting room is full of mostly elderly men and women, their faces lined with age. A few wear glasses, many are leaning on sticks. Their dusty clothes signify long walks through the bush to get here. Some are thin, their bodies showing evidence of malnutrition, or illness. On many of them their clothes are tattered and torn, giving notice of the poverty that also afflicts them. Some of the men wear frayed suits, remnants of a time when they had been more prosperous. The old women's chitengis have faded with age and from repeated washing.

These are starkly different to the bright peacock colours of the clothes the young women wear as they wait with their children outside the clinic door. Clinic day is a chance for them to show off any finery they possess. They meet with friends, and with rivals. There is noise everywhere, more muted tones from the elderly, shriller tones from the women and children, and lower tones from those who wait for the dentist at the door of the Tithandizane room.

There are mostly men at this door. Old and young they talk and wait. Some in smart dress, others in worn work clothes as they come from the fields to get an offending tooth removed. Some are holding their jaws as if at last they can acknowledge the pain that besets them, now that a chance of release is at hand. The dentist is inside the room, organising his equipment. He is well organised; everything is being well sterilised in a portable autoclave. He has enough equipment to deal with patients in blocks of ten. Ten waiting for the injection to take effect, while the previous ten have their teeth removed.

I am relieved that Amrita spends most of the day being the dentist's assistant. I just have to take over for a short time. I am extremely glad that I had my tooth out before I came to Zambia. Now I know in gory detail how it's done – at close hand. Not that he is a bad dentist, and he does have anaesthetic, it is just being so close to the act, and seeing such a number of teeth being pulled in a day. There is no time to do fillings. And anyway, by the time people come to the dentist their teeth, often several of them, are too far-gone to be rescued.

Tooth decay and the resultant infections are a source of ill health for many people in Zambia. It is a country that produces sugar cane, and which adores sugar, each person ladling many spoonfuls into their cups of tea. Numerous advertisement hoardings en route to the town extol the health and energy giving delights of sugar.

Once again I face calling out names.

"Ndanga?" I call, and look around.

I try again, "Ndanga?"

There is some shuffling and nudging, as a friend of the next "victim" understands my garbled version of the name. He comes to the door and I indicate the bench just inside.

I remember another word:

"kalopanze" "sit down".

It feels abrupt to say this; there is no word for "please" in this language, though "Thank you" "zikomo" is heard all the time.

I call the next and the next until there are five waiting expectantly on the bench. The meths burner is hissing in the background, steam pouring out, adding to the foetid atmosphere. It is past midday. It is hot, though not all the sweating is due to heat. The dentist is ready; he looks at the list and calls the first person to sit in the chair; an ordinary wooden chair that is beside him.

"Open".

He holds down the lower jaw and pokes and prods, sometimes evoking a grimace of pain from the victim. He barks out numbers at me to write beside the name, and then reaches for an awesome-looking needle attached to a syringe full of anaesthetic. He applies it close to the affected tooth, and sends the man back outside to wait.

"Next"

All five are prepared and sent outside to wait, the next are then called, dealt with and also sent back outside. The burner stops its sizzling. The instruments are ready. They are tipped into a sterile metal bowl. Time to call in the first five. Once again I have to try to get my tongue around the names, but they slip off it easier now. The five enter and sit down. The first one looks very reluctant to get back in the chair. I feel for him.

The dentist pulls on his gloves, looks at my list, looks in the man's mouth, seizes a shiny fearful looking instrument with forceps, then winces as the hot metal touches his hand by mistake. It is still hot from coming out of the autoclave.

He and the poor man in the chair have to wait a few more minutes. Then he turns back to the wide-eyed occupant of the chair. He holds the man's head, putting it into position and tells him to be still and open his mouth wide. He jiggles the offending tooth back and forth. I can barely watch. Then he is holding it up before me, or rather he holds up what remains of a tooth, a black, bloody stump. He puts it in a metal dish and slings the used instrument into a tray ready to be sterilised for another victim. He presses cotton wool into the hole, and presses the man's hand to his jaw to hold it there so that it will staunch the bleeding. He removes his gloves to count out some antibiotics and a few panadol to ease the pain (though not all have this luxury);he gives instructions not to eat for a while, and sends the man away; job done.

I feel a bit sick. I am glad I am not too squeamish, as this scene is to be repeated again and again. Sometimes too I have to actually hold someone's head when it is a difficult extraction. Above all I feel sorry for the others who are waiting on the bench in the room, witnessing what they too will have to endure. I am amazed by the courage of most of the sufferers, both before, when they must have been living with pain for a considerable length of time, and after, as the anaesthetic wears off. Some who had a particularly tough extraction are sent over to our house to rest before they tackle their long walk home.

The dentists' time is limited, so he squeezes in as many people as possible. He has got a lift from the opticians and has to leave when they are finished. They all come from a hospital a long way away. He works, as fast as possible, but at the end of the day there are still some who will have to wait till next time.

What a day!

It has been delightful meeting some of the people who had thought they would be blind for the rest of their lives, and now can see. At the end of it, sixty-seven people saw the dentist and seventy-eight the opticians. While countless numbers attended the clinic and yet more came to get advice from Amrita and Ndwali.

Helping people gain access to the opticians and dentists is only part of our work. The number of callers to the house is increasing. Often people are waiting before our 6am rise.

Last week Amrita had a meeting with a specialist at one of the hospitals, where they had discussed the problems of AIDS that lay behind many of the callers' visits. There is little medical treatment available aside from drugs to combat the TB, which often accompanies AIDS. Recently they are finding TB in the lymph nodes as well as in the lungs. There are some antibiotics for infections, and some simple analgesics such as panadol and aspirin for the pain. There is nothing to help the candida, or the herpes virus - the "shingles" that takes a long time to go away and is so often the first indication that someone may be harbouring the AIDS virus.

This doctor sees the importance of encouraging the cultivation of a wider range of vegetables to build up the immune system, and for all to try to purify the water they are drinking. They, and we, also talk about some dilemmas that face many working with people with AIDS. In particular we have been starting to suspect that an AIDS diagnosis actually hastens death. Recent figures are starting to indicate that life expectancy is greater if the person has not been given a diagnosis. But it presents a difficult moral dilemma. If one suspects AIDS, and does not voice suspicions, and a person is HIV+, they could carry on infecting others. And many people are starting to come. People suspicious they may have contracted HIV, are starting to come for advice from Amrita. It is becoming known that she is somewhat of an expert in the field. It is a dilemma that we each have to resolve in our own way.

Amrita does have useful knowledge. She has discovered, growing in Zambia, the healing bush "saboodang" (Latin name *Jatropha gossypifolia*), which is well known for boosting the immune system and is often used in fighting lymphatic leukaemia. This plant is also found in Thailand, where Amrita had spent time working with people with AIDS. A tea is made from its roots. She is also brewing another kind of tea, kwambucha, which has again been used in other countries and had been sent to Amrita by a man in America. Yeast and a fungus produce a tea rich in vitamin B complex, a good detoxifying tonic in the fight against illness. Extra vitamins and minerals and advice on diet and lifestyle could greatly increase quality of life, and give a greater life expectancy.

There is also a lot of fun and laughter in our work to get a serious message across. To help raise awareness of the prevalence of AIDS and how it is transmitted, as well as showing how it can be avoided, Amrita goes out on World Aids Day dressed as a condom, riding round the villages on a bicycle to promote their use. We are also promoting use of the femidom, a female condom, which had only been developed a few years previously. It has newly arrived in this part of Zambia. It could be particularly useful by enabling women to take more control of their health.

Awareness particularly needs to be raised in the women because sexual activity in Zambia differs somewhat from that in most other countries. They are used to having dry sex, the women very dangerously using herbs to dry out their vaginas. This leads to internal abrasions allowing the AIDS virus easier entry into the blood. Femidoms do start to gain in popularity with more young women as they begin to take charge of their health, but this is a slow process. However, some of their partners are also intrigued by the femidom, and we encourage them to try them out. I share a lot of laughter with people, as I try to explain to both men and women how they work. They come back for more, so they must have worked.

Sex is no taboo here. It is one of the enjoyments of life. There is little incidence of rape or child molestation though sexual behaviour starts very young and girls can be married after their menses start; from as young as twelve.

But sadly there are ever-prevalent sexual diseases, of which AIDS is only one. It is the prevalence of all the sexual diseases such as gonorrhoea, syphilis, chlamydia, trichosomonas that have in part enabled AIDS to spread like wildfire. The injuries that the diseases cause to the body leave open wounds that facilitate easy entry of the AIDS virus. Because there are few medical facilities outside towns, the diseases have just been stoically borne and left untreated. Part of the problem too is getting all their sexual partners treated at the same time and many do not want to tell their partners.

There are a number of reasons why AIDS has spread so rapidly in this country. The first warnings about AIDS went unheard and were not publicised. This allowed the HIV virus to spread widely. Also condoms are not used because their usage implies that the other person could have a disease; or that this is just a casual relationship, not a serious one. Also, because of the preference for dry sex, lubricated condoms are disliked, and viewed with much suspicion. A commonly held myth is that the lubrication actually spreads HIV.

There is much work to be done in helping the people reconsider their sexual practices. But first friendships have to be built so that the practices can be talked about, and the myths around the use of condoms voiced and dispelled.

There are also the babies. In the West, HIV+ mothers are advised not to breast feed, in order to prevent transmission of HIV. In Zambia, lack of safe water and difficulty with sterilisation of bottles mean that even if there is an HIV+ diagnosis, it is still better to breast feed. Seeing an "AIDS baby" is often a sad indicator that the mother is infected.

In fact figures quoted by Chiswa Kabuse of the Pan African News Agency in October 2000, show that in Zambia, while the majority of men are mostly diagnosed and dying in their late thirties, women are dying in their late twenties.

The hospital trips go on almost daily for one or other of us: taking people in the hope of treatment, bringing home others after treatment and also bringing some home some for whom treatment had failed. One evening sticks particularly in my mind, as it bears out the desperate need for more work to be done raising women's awareness of health issues.

I am at the hospital, for the first time without either Amrita or Ndwali, collecting patients returning home. I go, as usual, to the front entrance where the people I had taken in earlier wait for me. As they get the in the vehicle, a stranger, a sad-faced, middle-aged man, approaches me and tries to communicate something. Eventually he manages to convey that there is another patient who needs to return home to one of our villages. He guides me round the back of the outpatients and emergency buildings to an entrance that leads to the wards. There he begs me to wait. I sit in the vehicle waiting, wondering who will emerge. After a little while I see him returning pushing a wheelchair in which there is a small figure.

A child or an elderly woman, I wonder. But as I see her more closely, I realise she must be about my age. He lifts her awkwardly out of the wheelchair into the back seat of the truck. I go to help, but she shrinks from me. She points to the area of her left breast. A nurse then steps forward, explaining that cancer has eaten most of her breast away, she is in extreme pain, made worse by any physical contact; she is going home to die.

I drop off most of our patients close to their homes then turn to her husband for directions. He guides me to a village far out in the bush. I stop the vehicle where he indicates and get out of the vehicle. As I see him struggling to lift her out of the back seat I notice her mute fear and pain. So I step forward and take his place, lifting her carefully down. She weighs very little; it is as if I hold a child in my arms. I carry her tenderly, carefully, and walk across the village into her house.

She is very light, but grows heavy as I carry her. Trying not to cause her hurt and fearing dropping her onto the sandy soil, with great difficulty I traverse the distance to her home. Then we have to negotiate the low narrow entrance to her single-roomed hut.

What I see shocks me. The room is totally bare, not even a mat, as if waiting for a coffin, rather than for a living body. I have never felt such silence. Her family sit around the sides of the room, saying nothing as we enter. I gently put her down on the floor in the middle of her bare room trying not to add to her pain. I hold her for a little while after putting her down, my arms around her small shoulders. Before I leave, we look into each other's eyes, there are no words, but I know she feels the love that flows between us. She has at least returned with dignity and kindness. There is often nothing more than that to offer.

I will never forget that night. I will never forget the feeling of her in my arms.

The work with women's groups is desperately needed. Amrita is linking up with them and giving them encouragement. We meet up with one group in Mkolna village. They welcome Amrita with a wonderful song and dance session, before getting down to a serious and sensitive discussion about the realities of the sexual practices, and their dangers.

Via interpretation and sign language, we find out that many different types of herbs are used, in many different ways, to dry up the vagina. Some are particularly dangerous, leaving the women open to cancers as well as contracting HIV more easily. Amrita is hoping that information and research from our work will result in an American foundation donating money for sewing machines and materials for groups like this to make clothing and crafts with health slogans, which will both pass on the health message and generate income for the destitute.

Back home she writes and collates the details. When she presents her research, the project eventually receives a grant and useful books that will enable many women's groups to spread information and help women to lead more sexually healthy lives.

Meanwhile, I am making more friends. I am detailed to be in the little library room. Some youngsters come in. They rifle the books looking furtively at the boxes containing condoms and darting looks at me as I work nearby. I try a smile, and a few tentative words - in English and Nyanja. A broader smile comes back to me and the friends nudge each other encouraging the other to speak. I return the smile

"We have other things here too" I say.

And rattle one of the boxes.

"Do you need some condoms?"

Ice broken, they are now eager and astounded when I count ten out into their hands.

"Come back when you need more – and bring your friends".

Many of the young people are keen to improve their English by speaking with me, and to help me learn to speak Nyanja, bringing me lists of words to learn each week - and leaving with their condoms. We have lots of laughs, and by opening up discussions I am able to provide them with the condoms they have actually come for, the advice they sometimes want, and to spread the safe sex message to those who have not heard. The young men especially keep coming for both books to read and advice on living their lives. This is youth education, so similar to the work I had been doing in Scotland.

The hope of the future here in Zambia lies in helping these young men and women to learn to keep themselves safe from the AIDS virus. As we talk, safe sex can come onto the agenda, myths dispelled, and condoms handed out. Usually, next time they visit they bring a friend, and the next time, and so on. The message spreads. Wherever I go, whether in the vehicle or on foot, my bag is always half full of first aid materials and half full of condoms. Again and again I am stopped, even in the dark as I walk or as I drive through the bush roads.

The building of friendships, and the manner in which Amrita and Ndwali sensitively handle sexual issues, has built up much trust within the community. More people are now going beyond their fears to tackle the problems face on and to take more care of themselves and their families. More and more people are now coming with their health problems to Tithandizane.

CHAPTER SEVEN

Friendship

Perhaps life sounds rather grim; in many ways it is not. There is more laughter here, more community, and above all more peace. There is little violence and even fewer arguments. I feel safer here than anywhere I ever have been as an adult in Britain. And the scenery has its own beauty, especially as the sun rises and sets. This morning on the eastern horizon the redness of the sunrise offsets the darkness of the trees as if the sky is on fire. People help each other, in the villages especially. Here I am finding true friendship.

Friendship. One began the day I arrived in Zambia, when Mike met me, with Amrita and Gotami at Lusaka airport. This friendship is sealed a couple of weeks into my stay in Zambia when I answer an urgent call to go to him because he is close to death.

I had learnt about his battle with AIDS on the long journey from Lusaka to Tithandizane.

Brian, Mike's brother, is waiting at our house at 6am one morning desperately worried. Mike is very sick: vomiting and diarrhoea are racking his body, his temperature is high, he is delirious and in pain.

Brian is frightened, on the edge of panic so I promise to go with him. But the vehicle is away with Amrita.

"How can I get to his house?"

Brian points to his bike.

I shake my head in horror.

"No."

Bicycles and me do not get on! I have a long history of falling off them and injuring myself; I am a danger to others and myself so I have never learned to ride one. Initially Amrita and Ndwali did not believe me. However, when I did try to ride one, soon after arriving at Tithandizane, I got so tangled up and wobbled so dangerously that they never let me try again.

Brian again points to the bicycle.

I look around helplessly, not knowing what to do; Esther is in the background following the broken English and sign language that constitutes our conversation.

"He wants you to ride pillion."

She smiles.

"What! I can't ride pillion. I'll fall off. I'm much too heavy, I've never ridden pillion."

The thought fills me with horror.

But there is no other answer. It is the only way to get me to his village in the bush; it will take much too long to walk and someone has to go to Mike, till Amrita gets back. I grab my little rucksack with some basic first aid kit, put it on my back and stand next to Brian, and the bike.

He points to the luggage rack on the back, a few small iron bars.

"Does he think that will take my weight?"

I look wild–eyed at Esther.

I stand on tiptoe astride the rack. He takes his place in front of me and puts his foot on one of the pedals. The bike wobbles wildly as I lower my weight onto it; Brian pushes at the pedals. Slowly they turn; and then the wheels. We are off. Fortunately the first stretch is on tarmac, and a little downhill, so we manage to get started on our wobbly way. I hold my breath, not knowing whether I should go with the motion of the bike sideways as we go round bends or try to counterbalance it. I close my eyes as the occasional car or truck rumbles past us. I feel sick with fear. Not "car sickness", "bicycle sickness". Fortunately we do not tumble.

I feel sorry for Brian as he pedals; I am no lightweight. He even manages to talk a little in his limited English as we go along. He pours out his worries. Mike is the only breadwinner in the family, how can they survive without him? Mike is the oldest and most educated, his father is the headman of the village, what will happen to the family without Mike? Brian is a local pastor, but he, at not quite thirty, is relatively young and inexperienced. And scared!

We wobble again as we turn off the tarmac onto a dirt track; at first it is firm and the bike negotiates it quite comfortably, but all too soon it turns into pure sand which gathers in deep ruts. Brian puffs and pants, and eventually has to give up. He stops, and gratefully I get off. My legs shake. Tension had built up as I tried to avoid getting entangled with ground, wheels or pedals. It had been almost unbearable and the iron bars had bit into my bottom!

Fortunately we have not far to go, through the bushes I can see the outline of some grass-roofed huts. We walk along a well-trodden path, past a few fields and now some scrubland borders the track; a simple church is close by - Brian's church. We pass a few small dwellings and then turn into the village. Mike's house looks no different to the rest. A thatched grass roof supported by wooden poles set at intervals round the structure overhangs earthen coloured mud brick walls. A high, smooth, mud step borders the house underneath the overhang, and an open, rough wood door indicates the front of the house. A small opening high up under the eaves looks to be the only source of light apart from through the open door.

Some of his family sit silently on the step; while a couple of children play nearby. On the step a brazier holds a bubbling pot. A small, rather worn-looking woman, who is possibly close to me in age, comes out the door as we walk up. She gives a small smile and stretches out her hand, then immediately turns to Brian with a stream of questions in Nyanja. She looks worried, and he looks worried.

They motion me to go inside; I bend down to enter the small dark room. It is nearly empty, just a couple of chairs, a small table and a rush mat. They indicate that I should go through a curtained opening, into the second room. There, in near dark, I find Mike. The only furniture, his bed, takes up most of the room. Gingerly I sit down on it beside him.

"Modgala, where's Amrita?" He groans

"She will come later, with the vehicle",

I try to reassure him.

"Then we can get you into hospital."

"I'm dying".

He struggles to sit up, hands wildly searching for a basin. He retches, convulsive retching, which brings up little more than yellow phlegm; then sinks back, his brow covered with sweat.

"I have diarrhoea too, hasn't stopped for days - look at it..."

He motions Brian to get the pot that sits on the floor at the end of the bed.

"Are you drinking plenty of water?"

He shakes his head. "Can't keep it down".

"You must try. I have some ORS, blackcurrant flavour, ask Brian to get you some boiled water."

This type of ORS (Oral Rehydrated Supplement), has the balance of necessary salts in it, and is pleasantly flavoured. I hope it will encourage Mike to drink.

Brian returns with the water, and I mix up the solution. I persuade him to drink a little, but in his pain and delirium it is an effort. After a few sips he sinks back exhausted. I try to talk to him, but he is barely able to respond. His brother leaves us, and I talk and reminisce about our journey from Lusaka, remembering the fun we had as we searched for mangoes, his favourite fruit in the market, finally unearthing a couple of small green barely ripe apologies for fruit. I remind him of his determination to set up an HIV support group, and of his support Tithandizane, hoping this will give him the will to go on.

I lightly massage his thin body. Every part of him hurts. I have never felt someone so thin; I can feel every rib and every vertebra. There is hardly an ounce of flesh between skin and bone. I can almost get my fingers round his collarbones and underneath his shoulder blades. I gently stroke his smooth soft skin but even that is too much pressure for him so I just sit, holding him, waiting for Amrita.

Just being there comforts his mother too. When Mike dozes off, I leave him for a while with his brother, and go outside to sit on the step with his mother. We meet as two women: two mothers together, our mutual lack of language proving to be no barrier to our communication. Mid afternoon brings a welcome sound. The truck and Amrita has arrived.

We leave immediately for town to get Mike into the hospital. This is my first daytime visit to town. The first time I encounter the battle to get a patient to see a doctor. There is endless form filling, then it is time to get him settled in a ward.

It is my first sight of a Zambian hospital ward and it shocks me. I see row upon row of thin young men, some with families sitting by them, while others lie on the floor below the bed. Most often it is the mothers who are there to care for their sons, as Mike's mother is doing for him. My overall perception is of greyness. Pathetic looking bundles of possessions lie beside each bed, pots and pans and plastic plates for cooking meals in the communal kitchen, wrapped up in dusty chitengis. A grim silence prevails that speaks of suffering and sad acceptance.

There is little laughter here. We reluctantly leave him, hoping Mike will get some useful treatment, not least of all a drip of life giving water. For the moment there is nothing else we can do.

We go back the next day to see how Mike is doing. He is much the same, no treatment has been received and he has had enough. He wants home, and he is determined to go home. The only answer is to take him. He is a determined man, and we are not there to force others to stay, or go; and perhaps there is wisdom in wanting to die in his own home. We fear for him as we leave him at his home village, expecting to receive the worst news.

The next day Amrita returns to Mike's house. He is still alive but barely conscious, so she brings him back to the clinic. He lies there moaning, no longer able to take in water from a cup, his breath is hot and laboured. But there on the floor of the Tithandizane room he is at last drip-fed some life-giving water. We eventually go to bed; all of us fearing for his life, leaving him on the edge of life and death accompanied by his brother who is pacing and waiting.

Miraculously Mike makes it through the night, and next morning is ready to try another hospital. We visited this hospital en route as we came from Lusaka. Now I am to have my first drive in this direction on the potholed road. This time I am more aware of the stunning views across the bush to the distant hills. The hospital takes Mike in to have more checks and once again we have to leave him fighting for his life.

The life of someone living with AIDS is a series of ups and downs, raised hopes and dashed ones. Every day we fear a message arriving, telling us the worst, but once again Mike's indomitable spirit wins through. His determination to see Tithandizane safely established, and an AIDS support group set up, is I think, helping him to stay alive.

We speak much in Buddhism about will. Here I see it in action. Mike's determination inspires me, while his courage astounds me. A few days later when we return to his hospital with another group of patients, all of whom are admitted, we go to look for Mike and find him, though weak, very much alive. He is allowed to go provided he returns the following week for an ultrasound scan to look at lumps, which can be felt in his stomach area. We take him home to his delighted family.

His mother grabs my hand, and at last I start to see her true character. No longer serious, she now laughs and jokes. I can see her laughing at me. She sees me struggle to keep on my chitengi, the colourful cloth that I try to tie round my waist to form a protective skirt as the locals do.

I keep giving rise to much laughter again and again in the local campus and around the villages as my inadequately wrapped chitengi keeps falling down and floating to the ground behind me as I walk! It is, however, a very practical garment, protecting my suits from the bare earth I so often have to sit on. I have even found one in our Amida colours, with red flowers like lotuses.

Mike's mother puts her hands round my ample waist and deftly twisting the cloth firmly tucks it in. Then she makes me practise again and again, laughing all the while, until finally I get the hang of it!

At mealtime she shows me how to eat properly, demonstrating how to roll the mealie meal dumpling into balls with the fingers of my right hand, without plastering it all over the hand and anything else I come into contact with. A deft motion is needed, and then it needs to be dipped into the relish in a way that picks up enough to get a taste of it into the mouth. She is very kind. When our visits coincide with meal times, she finds us something to eat and even makes a vegetarian dish on the rare occasions they are eating meat or fish.

One day she really gets me laughing! This time when we arrive, after some delighted greetings, she looks at me and mimes a digging motion.

"You should be out in the fields," Mike translates.

We all laugh.

"Yes," I retort,

"but I haven't got muscles like yours!"

I indicate her slim and wiry arms and compare them with my round flabby ones. However they aren't quite as round and flabby as when I arrived perhaps I have lost some weight and built some muscle.

"And anyway, who will drive the vehicle?" I challenge.

"I will!"

she offers, while laughing and shaking her head. Few people from these bush villages can drive and even fewer are women.

This becomes a wonderful ongoing joke. We share much laughter together when we meet.

We meet frequently in the months to come; mostly we sit on the mud step and as we do the family gather round. Here I also acquire the name that is to be given to me by more and more children as time goes on. "Ambuya"; "Grandmother". I feel an enormous honour. This is my first step into the third age, which also feels like a coming of age, here in Zambia.

Mike's next trip to hospital shows up the lumps in the lymph glands, suggestive of TB. A biopsy is advised to check it out. Then, and only then, treatment can start.

A hard decision lies ahead of Mike; to operate on his skeletal frame is a risk but if he refuses, he might lose a chance of regaining some of his health. If it does prove to be TB, it is treatable. X-rays might have given a clearer picture, but the hospital has run out of film so the decision is put off. He needs time anyway to try to eat well and build up his physical strength. There is a hope too that another hospital might have X-ray film and thus offer better grounds on which to make a decision.

TB is a large and growing problem. Riding on the back of AIDS, it is giving additional complications, and often, unsuspected, untreated cases are very infectious, especially to those with lowered immunity. We are all watching out for possible indicators in the people we meet, so as to advise those people suspected of harbouring it to get tested and treated.

Nearly a week later Mike gets X-rays done at another hospital; however doctors give conflicting advice which only muddies the picture further, as the X-rays do not indicate clearly whether he has TB in the lungs.

A week later we are taking people for optical treatment to another hospital even further away from Tithandizane. Mike and Paula, another patient and friend, decide to come with us to see a doctor about their AIDS-related problems.

Mike's strength is increasing day by day. Alongside the good food and vitamins and minerals, the small amount of precious anti-candida medicine that Ndwali has managed to obtain in Lusaka, have contributed to his further improved health. My treasured filter cup has also been given to the cause, so that he can avoid drinking the contaminated water, which is all that is available in his home village.

It is wonderful to see the difference in Mike compared with how he had been a few weeks earlier, when his kidneys were not working properly due to the dehydration. Now he is trying to see if he can get the TB drugs without having the biopsy. He does not get the drugs at this hospital and this visit makes him more resolved to take his father's advice to try to avoid the biopsy.

While there Mike and I visit the little market beside the hospital. His appetite has certainly returned. Here in the shade of the tall trees that guard the hospital entrance I have my first taste of fresh boiled maize. I had expected the sweet taste of corn on the cob, which I am not terribly keen on - but this is different; these cobs have a mild, rich, almost nutty flavour that lingers in the mouth long after eating. Mike, after we return home, goes from strength to strength, and one fine day Amrita even discovers he has "borrowed" her bicycle!

Nearly a week later I go to town with Mike. This is for a social visit. He wants a day out! We go to a café for a treat of tea and cake, something I had never expected to do, and least of all with Mike. At that little café, beside the busy road where they make maize cakes that melt in the mouth, Mike reveals his dreams - first to work a little again, and then to reclaim his children who he has heard are being neglected. We go to visit their mother in the café where she works. She is friendly enough. I cannot understand the protracted discussions, but I feel Mike's deep concern as we walk away.

Mike is trying to put his house in order while he has the strength to do so.

We visit the market that sprawls alongside the road and into the back streets. It is a kaleidoscope of colour. Second hand clothes of every style and colour are in abundance at all the stalls around its outer perimeter. Inner stalls sell everything from bread to boot polish. Covered stalls display small, neat piles of many different sorts of fruit and vegetables, some of which I have never seen before. Other produce is being sold by women squatting on the ground near the entrance this; though often smaller is also cheaper, probably from poorer land and more suitable for our shoestring budget.

Mike takes me round his favourite stalls. Piles and piles of pungent fish attract him; it is a favourite relish for many, and it sits alongside piles of dried caterpillars. Dried beans of many different varieties go into his shopping basket, and mine. A small cabbage and a few potatoes join them. I decline the okra, though it is a delicacy to him. I had heard graphic reports about its slimy, mucousy greenness when it is cooked the Zambian way - fortunately I only have to eat it a couple of times.

On the way back, at the side of the road, where they are much cheaper, we will get a few tomatoes and some of the delicious little bananas, that are cheap and plentiful here. Black ones, yellow ones, fat ones, thin ones; however my favourite are the green ones.

There are plenty of Mike's favourite mangoes too. It is coming to the height of the season. Ripe mangoes, of many different colours and textures are available - not my favourite fruit. Guavas, however, are a different story! When they become ripe I am immediately hooked.

The day of the Tithandizane AGM a couple of weeks later finds Mike in good form. There is hope growing that more will be done for people who are HIV+. A young man from a neighbouring village who is HIV+, is enthusiastically backing the idea of having an HIV club – a support group for those facing AIDS, and he will work alongside Mike to set it up. Mike has been a prime mover in the formation of Tithandizane, this AGM means a lot to him, because no matter whether he lives or dies, it offers hope for his people in the future.

The AGM is a real eye-opener for me. I am a bit bemused by all the preparations and the importance it is given. I know that meetings are the lifeblood of the community here; however I had not realised that they are not only just to meet with others for business, but also for pleasure and entertainment. The Tithandizane AGM, the first, certainly provides that.

On the day, more than sixty people attend, including headmen of many villages. It is a long day of many speeches. Although I can understand little of the spoken language, the body language says it all. People are happy and emotions run high. It all feels very positive. The aims and objectives of Tithandizane now seem well established.

All are ready for the entertainment that is interspersed with the speech making. It is entertainment with an ulterior motive. Here Amrita is in her element; she has deftly choreographed the young members of the Munagra drama group in their sketches about health issues. Sharp and funny they bring home the various messages expounded in Primary Health Care teaching, and especially the ones about safer sex. In one amazing sketch Amrita plays a very convincing fly, buzzing around contaminating all the food. However the best sketch of all comes from Amrita and Mike. They are playing two hungry goats tied up together. Back and forward they pull each other, running and butting all over the floor and beneath the feet of the onlookers both trying to get to piles of food. They eye the unobtainable food very hungrily, as they pull against each other, but the jam sandwich sits out of reach, until one finds the answer.

"Tithandizane," he cries. "We help each other," feeding Amrita one of the sandwiches. She nods her head and feeds him the other. Neither goes hungry.

Tithandizane, the hope for the future lies in helping each other.

The AGM finishes with live music and dance. Traditional Ngoma dancing that demonstrates allegiance to their chief. To the onlooker it is erotic and enthralling. The drums calling the tune as each young man struts his stuff with costumes flying as he thrusts his pelvis forwards. But the biggest roar from the crowd goes up as Amrita joins the scene. She cavorts with the best and steals the show.

At the end of the day, we leave a happy and exhausted Mike back at his home. In fact all go away happy and entertained, full of hope that Tithandizane will fulfil its promise. The vehicle is commandeered to take groups of villagers at least part of the way home. The drummers take over the back of the vehicle, so that all the way there is literally "Dancing in the Street". The soft twilight enhances the scene; this is the end of a beautiful day, the sound of the drums forming a lingering lullaby as we go to sleep.

CHAPTER EIGHT

On the Road

...And now the dawn is rising, the cockerel crows and a new day begins. In getting to know the people and the villages I feel safe to walk alone from village to village to visit them, knowing there are friends to accompany me as well as making new friends. There is something wonderful about this walking from village to village. So often it brings me closer to knowing the Buddha's teaching. I can almost feel the heat he walked in and imagine his meetings and conversations. I see time and time again the ox carts and the oxen working, probably similar to what he saw. And in the people's waiting and even longing for the rains to begin in earnest and help the crops grow, I can imagine the rains retreats to which his followers returned each year after their travels. The Buddha comes alive for me here.

It starts with Ndwali's "Grandmother's aunt". I begin to get an inkling of how I can help ease the pain many suffer in a practical way. I have some problems with arthritis, and have in the past suffered from back problems and migraines. I have learnt to deal with the pain by heat and massage and have also done some simple massage on others. I wonder whether it might help here. So I have a go. She is delighted. I don't know whether it is the actual massage, or the gentle attention. Anyhow her smile says it all.

One Sunday, soon afterwards, I go out with Amrita and Gotami to visit some villages, Amrita pushing the bike through the sandy bush tracks, its basket full of medicines and condoms. For her it is a short walk, for me it feels rather a long one. As we reach the first village, people throng around us asking for advice. She helps some with first aid and advises others to go the clinic, or to hospital. She also hands out condoms and the vitamins and minerals that are much needed to boost the steadily deteriorating diet, as in the arid dryness, the fresh fruit and vegetables have run out.

Getting the clinic operating has led to the pregnant mothers, small children and babies getting the official supplements, but others will soon suffer the effects of malnutrition. It is the beginning of the annual downward health spiral. This is the start of the time of hunger, when the produce from one harvest starts to run out; ahead lie many months of sheer survival before the next crops are ready for harvesting.

This year is a particularly bad one. Last year the rains failed to arrive and there is not enough maize in store anywhere. This is going to be a hungry winter and spring.

We are doing all we can to help boost health before the deterioration starts in earnest. Already there are attacks of malaria and many suffering from pneumonia and other respiratory infections. Some come with accidental injuries, others with infected wounds and bites. The heat of the sun, malaria and effects of carrying heavy loads on the head give rise to a word I come to know well – "mutu" - headache. Here Amrita thinks I might be able to help a little; perhaps a few people will be open to trying massages rather than the ever cried-for panadol. She sends a woman over to me.

"Mutu oowawa".

This is graphically accompanied by very expressive grimaces and hands over the head! Looks like a bad headache!

I nod, and point to the ground, getting down there too. She looks a bit puzzled but sits down. I move behind her and hold her head between my hands.

It has been a while since I last gave a massage. That was more than six months previously, in my last job before I joined Amida, when I was supporting a young middle-aged woman who was suffering from an extremely painful, terminal illness. I think of Ina as I start to work. Ina is just a few years younger than I am; all the painkillers she stuffs herself with cannot assuage her pain, and some nights all I could offer to her was this gentle touch to help her sleep. We both cried when I left to join the Amida Order. However, by letting me go she has been able to offer a gift to others. She is with me in spirit as I start this work in Zambia.

I feel the head that I hold in my hands. This is a very different head to Ina's. Ina had long thin hair, small skull and a bony face. Here I feel short, rough, crinkly hair and a very rounded head. My fingers explore the ridges and hollows; they feel the taut muscles in her neck, the furrows of pain in her forehead. I breathe in and focus my attention on her as she sits on the ground in front of me.

I ease my already aching knees into another position to explore further. My fingers caress her cheekbones, easing out the tensions, then drift towards the ears, gently pressing on the bony protrusions behind them. I pinch the edges of the ears, then slowly make my way down to the nape of her neck. Here I stop a little and feel out the structure, my fingertips searching for any knotted muscles, I probe on, releasing knots until her neck feels more relaxed and flexible. Smoothly I move onto her tense shoulders, I squeeze and loosen, pulling her shoulders back into a more natural position. For a final minute I hold her there, my hands lying lightly on her shoulders till it is time to release her to go on her way.

As she gets up, I realise that I have an audience, and a queue. The watchers are fascinated. Massage is totally new to them. My first client moves her head around, feeling the new lightness, and her smile of pure pleasure and relief encourages others to give this a try. Others now come with various aches and pains. Someone finds a chair. It is much easier than kneeling behind someone on the ground. I am very grateful. That afternoon seems to go on forever as women come with limbs swollen and sore from arthritis.

I remember sitting before Ina in her wheelchair. I remember Ina's small soft hands with pointed fingertips and nails misshapen by her illness. I remember her thin bony ankles. Here as I sit in the dust before an elderly woman, I feel square work-worn hands with knuckles out of shape from arthritis. The next person displays an ankle that is grossly swollen, dirty and dusty from a long walk through the bush. They keep coming and keep smiling as they leave, loving the new experience.

Ina also had never experienced massage before my arrival at her home, she found it deeply calming, and was touched by the love that flows through both the one being massaged and the masseuse. There is an exquisite tenderness in it, and here in Zambia it is no different.

Darkness is falling on that first day of walking in the villages. Gotami is given a lift back on someone's bike. Amrita and I walk home in a leisurely fashion, accompanied to the tarmac road by friends from the village. In the coming months I rarely walk alone. The code of friendship and hospitality means that we are accompanied at least part of the way. As we walk we talk, and people start to share their concerns as they try to draw this stranger into their society. They talk with honesty and openness:

"The biggest problem here is jealousy."

"These illnesses are due to curses put on because of jealousy".

I hear similar observations again and again. Even in a community that has little, there is still much that can give rise to jealousy and raise old beliefs in magic and mystery. The more I learn more about people's hopes and fears and the way they make sense of the health problems and poverty they experience, the more I am drawn into the life of this community and start to learn how many people make sense of the disasters that are befalling them.

In the villages more and more people call for my services. I start to go further afield, sometimes in the vehicle, and sometimes walking.

In a far-off village I meet a young woman. Slender and pretty, she sits on the mud step of her home and smiles a tentative smile as I approach. I can see that her joints are very swollen and painful and her knees are bent up to her chest. I go to sit on the step with her while Amrita and Ndwali question her. She lives bent up like this - permanently. For twelve years she has been in this condition and has never seen a doctor because her family say it is too far to travel. Amrita looks at her limbs, examines the swelling, and sees how she winces in pain at any attempt at movement. Amrita searches for some anti-inflammatory pills, and explains to Anna how to use them.

I also gently explore Anna's limbs, feel the foreshortened tendons behind her knees, and know that there is little we can do to help her regain the mobility lost. However we can help slow down deterioration and ease the pain. We surmise that it is untreated rheumatoid arthritis. Today I just hold her painful limbs, cupping her hands and wrists, feet and ankles between my hands. I promise to return to help loosen those joints a little, and to start giving her the care she has never received. We are to learn later that prior to our visit she had been shut away, forgotten and forlorn.

A week later I revisit Anna. The swelling has reduced a little and I am able to continue the massages that will gradually give her a little bit more flexibility and less pain. Though frustrated to see the neglect, I cannot blame her family; she lives in a very poor village, far from the road, where there is a feeling of desertion and desolation. I notice too that there seems to be much sickness in the village and the usual sound of children's laughter is absent. The children's swollen bellies testify to the bad water supply, and lack of latrines. The apathy there is palpable.

In another, very different village - Mkolna - I am introduced to the headman by Joseph. In this village there is a more vibrant atmosphere. I went there recently with Amrita to visit the women's group when we were interviewing them about the use of vaginal drying herbs. In this village more people are taking action to improve their conditions. This is Joseph's village, and Joseph certainly believed in taking action. His encouragement and support of Tithandizane speaks for itself.

Now I am meeting the headman; I am expected, Joseph has been advancing my services. I walk forward to meet the tall thin, elderly man with bushy white hair who is sitting in a deckchair underneath the overhanging thatched roof outside his front door. After Joseph makes the introduction I step forward holding out my hand. He takes it and shoots at me a flow of Nyanja, then sees my perplexed look and turns to Joseph demanding that he explain.

"He had an operation on his back twelve years ago. It did not work and he has been in constant pain ever since."

"Can I have a chair?"

Joseph looks a bit surprised, I guess what he is thinking, it is not done to ask for a chair for oneself. I smile.

"No, it is for him"

Joseph still looks bemused, but sends for a chair. The headman looks on, asks Joseph something, and I can see that Joseph is indicating that he does not understand. I smile at them both. The chair arrives. Good, it is a useful one.

"Zikomo" - "Thank you", I say.

Now I have to somehow explain how I want the headman to sit on it. I explain to Joseph that I will demonstrate. I hitch up my trousers and sit astride the chair, leaning on my arms, which are resting on the back. I turn and look back at the headman,

"Please can you sit like this?"

He gets up awkwardly. I can see that his back is curved grievously. He manages to sit astride the chair, uncertain of this strange new posture.

I find a suitable log and sit behind him. I call on Joseph to be interpreter again.

"Can you tell him that I need his jumper pulled up so that I can look at, and feel his back?"

The headman does this, and I study the knobbly backbone, then feel my way up and down. I can see the long thin white scars from his operation and the gross curvature of his spine. I share my observation that I don't think there is a lot I can do to help, but some massage might ease the pain. I move slowly and gently up his back, my fingers either side of his spine. They search for tense and knotted muscles, working at them and smoothing them. I knead the muscles over his ribs with the joints of my fingers and rub and press with the heel of my hand. His back feels a little more flexible now, so, massage over, I ask him to stand.

I am not sure whether to do the next thing, but decide to have a go. I demonstrate a few simple standing exercises that can help flexibility and ease pain; he stands in front of me watching. He and our surrounding watchers find this highly amusing, but watch intently anyway. My friend Joseph interprets my instructions carefully. The headman attempts some of these standing exercises, and assures me he will do them regularly; I must admit I wonder whether he will.

However I return a week later, and with wonderful mime he demonstrates that he has been doing them; his eager welcome demonstrates that at least I have been of some use. As time goes on, he is to say that the night after my visits is the only time he gets a good night's sleep.

Joseph is always keen to learn; to try out different ideas and direct people my way who he thinks I may be able to help. He is also my teacher, keen to give me advice, telling me about the social norms, instructing me how to behave, and warning me about things too.

He takes every chance possible to instruct me. I will always remember travelling with him in the truck when I was newly arrived. We were talking as the light faded returning him and others to his village. I remember and can still feel the turn of my stomach as he made it abundantly clear that if I am to be trusted, I will need to stay - and if I did not, the people would be unlikely to trust another. His words firmly echoed those of the MP's wife.

"Besides", he says, "You might as well die in Zambia as anywhere".

Tough words, but true. What does it matter where one dies? There is however much more likelihood of dying in Zambia. Snakes are always a danger even more so out in the bush and also contracting diseases if I am not careful about water. Even in hospital, though there are good doctors, there are few medicines available, and if I ever need blood I fear that there is a large chance I will contract the AIDS virus from it. And the malaria season approaches.

One day the headman asks me to visit a woman who lives nearby and who is very sick. After giving him his massage I go to visit Joseph and to ask him to be my interpreter. As always, word has preceded me about my presence in the village, and as so often happens, a meal is ready and waiting. Even in the times of direst hunger I am stunned by people's generosity in providing food when they think we are hungry, that is if they have it to give. Afterwards Joseph comes with me to visit the sick woman.

As we approach the hut, Joseph recoils.

"I can't go in there,"

I don't understand, "Why?"

"It's my mother-in-law!" Joseph replies.

Oh dear, I have found out the hard way about another tradition and taboo. Men, I find, are not allowed to be in the same room as their mother-in-law for a large number of years. I guess it can prevent many dilemmas in their relationships. There is no way round it, Joseph is adamant; I have to find another interpreter. However I learn from my embarrassment. It reminds me that I have much to learn about the way of life here and that I must not become over-confident.

Joseph is a frequent companion as I tread an ever-increasing number of kilometres going from village to village. I am introduced to many people wanting massages and basic medical care as well as time to talk, teach and share.

At first we walk through fields that are dry, dusty and empty which look incapable of growing anything. As the weeks and months pass we walk in between rainstorms, picking our way through mud, and watch the green shoots of cotton, groundnuts and maize appearing.

One memorable day, just before Christmas I hear the sound of carols in Joseph's local church. He invites me in and I sit a little while, enjoying the glorious sound. It is lovely to hear the voices rise in praise, in that beautifully simple tiny church. No pomp and circumstance just songs and prayers expressing the joy of being alive.

I find my walking legs. Most days I set off joyfully to do some of my increasing round of home visits. I rarely walk alone. Quite often I am accompanied by some of the young people and our discussions tackle an enormous breadth of subjects from life in Britain, our communities and societies, to their prospects in Zambia and the fear of AIDS. We talk of our differences and our commonalties, our mutual difficulties and joys.

As they learn from me all they can, I learn from them - these, the bright hopes of Zambia's future as they try to teach me about their language and their culture. At other times some of the women, quite often the teachers from the school, stroll with me for distances along the way enjoying conversations and comparing our lives.

It draws me closer to the people when they see that I, like them, can tread the dusty bush roads in all weathers. I soon can easily walk fifteen kilometres in a day. It gives time to talk, and to learn together. They take care of me too; when able they fill my pockets with food, especially mangos. As the demands on my time grow, again and again darkness is falling while I am still miles from home.

One memorable evening, darkness has fully fallen, when a man accosts me on a bicycle – insisting that he gives me a lift home. I try to decline. After all, although I am no longer the fat woman who first arrived in Zambia, I am still no lightweight; also I know that the track and the road run mostly uphill! However he insists, and succeeds. Such is the hospitality in this corner of the world.

Another time it is Ndwali who comes out looking for me. He takes this chance to point out to me that the villages I walk to are only part of the area that Tithandizane covers. To the West lie many very neglected villages. Recently he and Amrita have been visiting them, recording their observations of the needs of these villages and finding yet more people who need hospital treatment. However to my surprise, even in these outlying villages they have received a request for me to visit someone for massage. Word has spread, and I promise that in the New Year I will spread my activities further and start to teach others how to give the massages.

Hope also lies in the children.

In one village the children practise on me. One day, while I am waiting for Amrita, the children swarm around me. One is more daring than the others; she reaches out to touch my long brown hair - my hair fascinates the children. At last they have got the longed-for chance to touch it. They also want to feel the texture of my skin, so I guide their hands into massaging movements. I hope that one day some of these children might learn some of these skills to help others.

As time goes on and the constant wetness of the rainy season takes its toll, they also run to me displaying their sores, whenever I appear. When they see that I will not do anything until the sores are duly washed, they learn to come to me, their afflicted limbs dripping with water, ready for the antiseptic and the treasured plasters to be applied! It is in fact noticeable as the rainy season progresses that this simple care has prevented many from having the terrible tropical sores many children display in other villages. I love going to this village full of wonderful rowdy, lively children who became my rumbustious, quarrelsome friends. Sadly it is also becoming a village of children and old people, as many adults in the prime of their lives, are dead or dying from AIDS.

However, I have many joyous walks home with these children who have also adopted me as "Ambuya." Often the children laughing and grabbing my hands help still the tears that have welled up inside me from caring for people who have untold suffering. They tease and mimic me as we chant and sing, walking home in the glory of the sunset. It is a wonderful walking meditation as they chant together with me their approximation of "Om Amitabha Hum" – my favourite mantra. I feel full of joy as I walk home in the fading light chanting it as the sun slips over the western horizon.

The fears I had before I came to Zambia fall into the background. This work takes me beyond my little "self": there is just no time to think about my needs, my worries. All the focus is outwards, both on people's needs, and on what they are trying to teach me. The focus is wider than the people too; the land itself seeps into my bones; my love of this country and for her people deepens.

CHAPTER NINE

Susan's Story

It is very ritualised, the whole process from death to burial. Waiting at the house the men sit outside, while inside the women sit in a room bare of all but mats, sometimes silent, at other times the chanting and wailing rises to a crescendo each time another mourner arrives. ...(Later) the long slow journey back to their home with the body is punctuated by hymns; behind me, the mother crying bitterly in her despair. Beside me sits the father; his silent tears are almost more poignant.

I first meet Susan the day the dentist and eye doctors come. When I finally get back to our house after my stint with the dentist, she is sitting in our room, leaning back against the wall holding her sleeping son. She is chatting animatedly with Monica, and is obviously at home here. She does however look very worn; a headache is troubling her, so Monica volunteers me to see if I can help.

I go and sit behind her and she stretches out her slender legs to take the weight of her son. She leans back against me as I run my fingers through her thick, yet soft, curly hair. I turn my attention to her high forehead and well-defined cheekbones, gently stroking the pain out from them. My fingers are searching for taut and knotted muscles. She sighs as the pain starts to slip away. In our shared smiles a friendship is born.

She has brought her baby son to the clinic because he is suffering from a fever. He keeps being unwell - repeated attacks of malaria the clinic says. Her husband George is often around the site and sometimes acts as my interpreter when I head off with the vehicle to visit bush villages; I have visited their house a few times after giving him lifts home. They have a relatively large house, with a corrugated roof and wooden veranda, quite close to the road.

George comes from a fairly affluent family so this house is quite comfortably furnished with soft seats, a proper dining table and photos around the wall. We sit there and have conversations that consist mostly of sign language. Where George has a fair command of English, Susan has very little however we manage to communicate well despite this and so our friendship grows.

Susan visits our house a week or so after the big day. The baby is crying piteously and burning hot. The nurse has not yet arrived, and there is a big queue outside the clinic. The poor baby sounds desperate, and Susan looks despairing, not knowing what to do with him.

She is exhausted, so while they wait to see the nurse I hold him, take off some layers of clothes and sponge him with lukewarm water to bring down his temperature. I remember doing this many times with my own children when they were small and suffering repeated bouts of tonsillitis. I am quite shocked to see how many babies are overdressed in this very hot climate. Also I am beginning to realise that most mothers do not seem to have any idea of how to bring down a temperature.

He feels fragile in my arms this beautiful child. He is not a young baby, and might be more than a year old. I have never seen him playing so I cannot tell. My heart aches at holding him, fearing for him, and longing for my own children. Their childhood seems a long way in the past.

Susan returns later with chloroquine from the nurse. She crushes the tablets in a spoon, and mixes the powder with water; and tries desperately to get him to take it, but as fast as she gives it, he spits or vomits it back up. I hold him as she spoons it into his mouth, and finally manages to get the chloroquine into him, as well as some medicines to ease the vomiting and bring down the temperature. Eventually he goes into a fitful sleep, and Susan is able to take her own medicine. She has malaria too. Once again she sits leaning against me as I massage her head and neck to give her a little relief from the pain.

Over the next couple of weeks we see quite a lot of George and hear of their desperate search for medicines to help their child. Nothing seems to help him. Finally we hear that he has been admitted to hospital because he is so weak. They are still hopeful of a cure. A few days later, knowing we have a trip to the hospital with patients coming up in a few days, I call into their house to offer mother and baby a lift home if they are ready to be discharged.

I am not prepared for the sight I find. I had not yet been inside a funeral house, and I am not prepared. I did not realised the baby was so sick. The house, which I last saw full of furniture, warm and welcoming, is stripped bare. All the furniture is gone, piled up into one of the bedrooms. In the two main rooms the only things to be seen are rush mats. In one room a small group of women sit around the walls long legs and dusty feet stretched out before them. Some of them are covering their faces with cloths, and lean into them, wailing.

As I enter, the wailing grows to a crescendo and then dies down to a low keening. I take a place against a wall. Some women glance briefly at me but none of the women look at each other. We just sit, no words are spoken, there is just a haunting keening that from time to time rises and falls from each of the women there. Someone else enters, she is wailing loudly and almost falls as she collapses against the wall. Again the wailing increases into a crescendo of grief and then quiets a little until the next arrival.

We are united in grief. We are women together, mothers crying, at the fragile reality of life and death.

The mourners will stay for hours; some will stay the night, others for many nights; but I have work to do; there is a body to collect and a funeral to arrange.

The shape of the men's grief is different. A small grim-faced group of men sit outside under the tree talking quietly while George paces around, occasionally stopping for a few moments, gesticulating wildly. Then he recommences striding around and cursing. He is raging at the hospital for having let the baby die, all for want of a blood transfusion.

The baby has died from anaemia. This is a frequent cause of death in Zambia, as both malaria itself and the chloroquine used to treat it deplete the iron in the blood. Blood tests showed that he was just above the very low limit at which a transfusion will be given. As he speaks I sadly know that even if he had had the transfusion, the child would probably have eventually died anyway. Because of the HIV there is a terrible shortage of blood and a reluctance to give it unless it is going to be life saving.

George comes back with me to Tithandizane to ask Amrita if the vehicle can be used for the funeral. Yes, of course we will offer the vehicle to collect the body and carry him for burial. Ndwali is away at a training course in Lusaka and Amrita is responsible for an outreach baby clinic the next day, so I will be the driver. I arrange to collect George and the funeral party early next morning.

We set off early the next day for the hospital mortuary. En route, outside the family home the back of the pick-up fills with women of all ages, dressed in their bright chitengis, singing and chanting hymns that range from the mournful to the ceremonial. Their heads are covered in a variety of coloured scarves as they arrange themselves around the tiny coffin. Beside them is an odd shaped bundle - tied up in a chitengi are bowls and wash things and clean clothes in which to dress the body.

George sits beside me, not uttering a word. Large, slow tears slip down his face. We drive sedately down the potholed road, the long forty kilometres to the hospital, then slowly up the driveway. Instead of heading to the front door, like we usually do, heading for the outpatients and wards, we drive round the side to the mortuary entrance. I pull up in front of a small square grey building with large doors. George goes in; then shortly returns, and he and another man take in the tiny wooden coffin. A small group of women follows them, carrying the bundle containing the materials to wash and dress the child.

The rest of us sit around the vehicle to wait.

The sun shines. We talk a little and sit in the warmth of the sun, on a small piece of grass close to the mortuary doors. For me this is to be one of many such meditations outside mortuary doors; however this is different to most, here I am a friend of the family. When the doors open and the group of relatives start filing round to view the body and pay their last respects, I am motioned to join them.

Slowly and silently we walk round the tiny coffin. He lies there, beautifully dressed, looking as if he is just asleep. Then the coffin is borne into the back of the vehicle, the mourners surrounding it singing hymns to send the little one on his way. Tears flow.

It is one of the longest drives of my life, both literally and emotionally. Hazard lights blinking we creep out of the town. A little more normal speed is allowed in the intervening portion, but as we near their home area the pace slows again, the normal one-hour journey taking two slow hours. People stop to attention, looking to see who is in the vehicle. Their stillness offers their respect to the grieving family. Many cars also stop to let the sad cortege pass. All the while the mother is crying in a way I have never before heard - wails of grief that are almost beyond human sound.

We drive well past our clinic and turn off the tarmac onto a dusty bush road. We still have a long way to go. Susan comes from a village deep in the bush. It is there that the burial will take place.

Finally we stop as we enter a village. This is the village where Susan has been born and raised. Fresh wailing comes from the mourners in the back of the vehicle, while the wails of the mother intensify, joining those of the crowds gathered around a small square house. The people are waiting to send the little one on his final journey.

The tiny coffin is borne into the house of his grandmother, where yet more people file round it to pay their last respects. Not silently this time as their wails demonstrate their shared grief. Susan stays in the vehicle, her strength gone. I sit on the ground outside the house with a group of women, silently waiting.

Then comes the sound of a hammer on nails. An eerie sound. A final sound. This is the last straw for Susan she tries to get out of the vehicle but collapses hanging onto the door. She cannot even find the strength to follow the coffin carried by her family, as they walk into the woods to the grave. With guidance from some of the men I drive her in the vehicle, through the trees, following the slow procession, till finally we stop below the trees close to a gathered crowd.

It is getting hot. The crowd has entered the sparse woodland and surrounded a newly dug hole. A mound of earth, and a stack of branches await, ready to cover the little coffin. The people disperse into small groups over a large area as they seek the shade of the trees. Susan wails in the vehicle. A family member sits with her. She tries to get out, but again her legs buckle under her and she leans back into the seat where she can hear but not see the proceedings.

The line of mourners who follow the tiny coffin, take their places near the mound of earth. I join some of the women, finding a spot with a thin covering of grass and some shade that affords a little protection from the scorching sun. Some of the crowd of people spread out under the surrounding trees look towards the truck as if willing Susan to join them. She remains apart and for the moment is silent – waiting.

At the graveside, there in the middle of the woods, reigns a silent peace. Groups of people sit dappled by the sunlight that makes the women's chitengis look bejewelled. Most have wrapped their heads in scarves, some brightly coloured, others plain blue, white or black.

The sadness shared by the community in this silence is almost palpable. An elderly woman rises and calls all to prayer. The silences are now interspersed with beautiful singing and chanting, and readings by various members of the congregation. The elderly churchwoman directs the proceedings, and gives what sounds like a rousing sermon. The village headman or perhaps it is the Induna (the headman's advisor) also gives a serious, considered, speech to send the child on his way.

While more haunting melodies from the congregation fill the grove, the men take it in turns to put spadefuls of earth onto the coffin, until another, smaller, mound lies amongst the green and gold of the trees, bathed in shafts of sunlight. Then they pick up many branches from the pile laying the other side of the mound, and reverently place them on top, giving it a covering that will protect it from wild animals. After a final hymn people start to rise, and I return to the vehicle. It is time for another long slow drive, this time taking the mother and as many people as we can squeeze into the pick-up, back to her marital home.

I leave the grieving family at Susan's home. My work is done for now. Later that day Amrita and I visit again to pay our respects. We join the lines of women sitting and laying on the rush mats in the inner room, joining with the mother in her grief. As each person arrives she wails her grief then others join in, singing the sad song that speaks of many griefs known and shared. I am touched deeply by the wisdom of these shared rituals and hope they will help Susan go beyond the desperation and despair a mother undergoes on losing a child.

We call again a couple of days later. Funerals go on for days, and for weeks afterwards friends and relatives who have not been able to attend the funeral call to offer condolences, as is proper for them to do, in a protracted mourning process. They go on for as long as it is necessary for all to pay their respects, and for the bereaved persons to go beyond that sharp initial pain of loss and start picking up the threads of life.

However, there is a strange atmosphere in the house. I do not understand it, this is not my culture, but I feel apprehensive sensing that something is wrong. Seeing Susan I am concerned, I can see that she is silent and focussing inwards, mostly not relating to anyone around her. More than anything I sense that her family are very worried.

All I can do is sit and join them, and when she comes to me, massage her aching head. Her head feels so different to the last time back in our house. Her head is now totally shorn; a practise that is another ritual procedure designed to help the process of grieving.

A week after the funeral I call again. There are fewer people here now and they are mostly close family members. George is now able to join us. He sits beside me as I massage Susan's head. I feel her frail body against mine; I can feel that this once strong and elegant woman has lost hope and sunk into a pit of despair.

Her husband turns to me, "She will not speak, she will not eat, and she will not walk. She is like a zombie, living dead. She is shutting all out. Help us. Please, we don't know what we can do".

Her mother and family add their pleas to his. Even without George's translations I know the meaning of their words. I feel their desperation.

George knows that I have studied psychology. Perhaps too he knows that I have also lost a child. They can see that Susan's path through grief has gone awry. She is not grieving now like a normal African woman, allowing herself to be carried by the rituals into a place where death is accepted, acknowledged and allowed its' rightful place in their lives. Death is part of their lives. They live close to it all the time. They almost celebrate it; or rather celebrate the life that has been. Many children die. Practically no family is spared.

Susan has got lost in aloneness by her withdrawal from all and everything around her. She is alone with her grief. Perhaps they sense she is grieving more like a woman of the west, so unprepared for these disasters when they fall. Perhaps that is why they beg me to help.

"What can I do?"

How can I find words to encourage her, and rouse her out of her stupor? Whatever words I find would be further stilted by her husband's enthusiastic, but often inaccurate, interpretation. I sit with her. I cannot offer anything clever. I can only offer myself. I can only share my own experience; share woman to woman, mother to mother, that terrible grief one feels when ones child is torn away by death. Share the pain that is fortunately beyond all comprehension until it happens.

The desperation that occurs on losing one's child is almost impossible to describe. There is nothing one can do to change what has happened. One is face to face with death at its sharpest and the reality of the impermanence and fragility of life. In this place life is no longer worth living. Anger, guilt and pain fill the void.

I look within, remembering, searching for a response. I realise that, like me, when my son died, she has an older child. For my remaining child I went through the motions of living when all I wanted to do was die and join my son. For my daughter I ate, I walked, I spoke; and gradually I came back to life. I found the will to live.

I try to find words to share my story. By sharing it I just hope she too can find the will to survive.

I don't think my words even need interpretation. We know. I get up to go, feeling hopeless, useless, feeling the pain, hers and mine. She gets up with me. Sees me to the door.

"Goodbye."

The first steps. The first word. I dare to hope that she has found her will.

The next I hear is that she has gone away.

She stays away for a couple of months and then returns, full of her old vigour. A couple of months after that she supervises cooking for eighty at a workshop.

It is also likely that my being able to grieve together with Susan after her loss made me one of the wider community. In my sharing I am now no longer so strange to them. They can see, and would hear it on the grapevine, that I have suffered loss too, and survived. Through my own loss I was able to help one of them to come through that shadow and survive. People now start to trust me and welcome me in a different way, as a woman in their society. I am glad that I was able to help a friend.

In the next few months I make many more friends.

CHAPTER TEN

Adoption

It is very humbling, very moving to be made part of the family. To join in their laughter and their grief. We learn so much from each other. I also feel a deeply shared spirituality, beyond the labels of Buddhist, Christian, or whatever. There is a common goodness, kindness, open-ness. Love in action.

My relationship goes beyond friendship with one particular family. It is a kind of adoption. I am very fortunate that this family takes me under their wing, to help teach me the ways of their society. This is the family of Ndwali. This teaching starts on the day I arrive when I first meet Ndwali, and it continues until the day that we say goodbye, in Lusaka airport.

I come out of the house one morning, soon after arriving at Tithandizane and see a stocky, middle-aged man deep in conversation with Ndwali. His trousers are tied to his legs with bicycle clips. He carries a bag and close to him I see a bicycle standing. I presume he had been travelling from a distance away, yet he looks as if he is ready for a business meeting. He spots me. He obviously knows who I am.

"Malka bwanji ?" He says.

"Good morning, how are you?".

"Naowko bwino; Kanamwe?" I reply.

"I am well, how are you?"

I am now able to offer the ritualised greetings.

"How do you find Tithandizane. Are they good to you?"

He fires questions at me, not rapidly, but seemingly with a determination to elicit honest answers. He then proceeds to give me what feels like a lecture about what is needed in the community, and what I should do. I feel like a senior elder is addressing me. Ndwali makes his apologies and leaves us; I have a suspicion that he is making his escape.

Mr Ndaka had been a head teacher locally, and though he lives in a village some distance from the Tithandizane area, he visits regularly en route to Chipata where he is building a house, and where more of his family lives. He is still teaching at a primary school close by his home village, and right from the very start is also intent on teaching me, particularly about the culture and the social laws that govern almost every action in the Ngoni tribe. I am enjoined to learn about their way of life and their complex hierarchical society.

I start to feel like one of the family. In fact one day Mr Ndaka says that they must be better than my own parents to me. That is their tradition and I must learn their ways, their traditions. It's interesting how many of his views echo those in Buddhist teachings. I left my family behind to live a life devoted to going where there is need. Now Mr Ndaka is enjoining me to know that wherever we are, is our home, and the people we are with are our families. That here I am his family.

In the Ngoni tribe the culture is hierarchical and patrilineal and has been less affected by the years of colonialism. Probably because it was less different in form than that of the indigenous matrilineal tribes whose views varied most with the colonisers. In matrilineal tribes the child's closest relative is the mothers brother and a man's heirs are his sisters children. It is the opposite in the Ngoni and life is often hard for women as they do not command respect, being treated like children, and trained to be wives who must accept their husband's wishes. However there are many strong women around. Including Mrs Ndaka.

One day I hear that Ndwali's mother is in the area, I had been told much about her and had never seen a picture of her. I recognise her immediately as she walks towards me. I don't know how I know but, without even thinking about it, I greet her,

"Malka Bwanje Mrs Ndaka?"

She looks amazed!

" Malka Bwino". She replies,

and turns to others around us exclaiming at my "second sight". It is a meeting neither of us ever will ever forget, and sets a seal on our friendship. The story is related at every family gathering, growing in the telling - I think. My understanding of Nyanja is still not good, but the laughs and looks say it all.

Mrs Ndaka stays with us that night, taking Ndwali's bed. The next morning I am up at first light doing my washing. A frequent chore as I have few clothes, and the red dust gets into everything, leaving deep stains if left for too long. In some ways cream is not a very practical colour to wear.

I sit on our veranda, rubbing at my clothes with the bright blue paste that is the favoured soap for washing clothes here. As I struggle to get out the stains, she watches, and then, finally unable to hold back, takes the clothes from me and shows me how to do it. She guides my hands into the right actions, scrubbing at every inch of material; then firmly wringing it out with her strong arms. She is a very strong woman, large in build and powerful in personality. Her word goes!

She is, however, also ready to learn. I teach her massage, and she is an enthusiastic pupil. She enjoys it practiced on herself, and also doing it on others, She takes the ideas home. When I next visit her village she has the women lined up for me to work on, watches my actions, and then has a great time massaging them herself - all amidst hearty gales of laughter.

I enjoy my visits to her house. There I have the rare chance of sleeping in a real bed, sometimes next to her. In the communal room we sit on low seats around a low table to talk and eat, though I grow to enjoy joining the women in the thatched roof cookhouse outside. Ndwali has several younger brothers, a young sister and also a wife and young son who form part of the extended family that squeezes into the house of Mr and Mrs Ndaka. In Ngoni society it is quite usual for wives to live either at the house of their in-laws or to have a house in the village whereas in the indigenous matrilineal tribes wives stay in their own villages.

The house of Mr Ndaka is square and has several bedrooms. It is large in comparison with most village dwellings. Its surroundings are kept neatly swept and planted, and many trees shelter it.

The village itself is also neatly laid out and clean and tidy. There is a different atmosphere in that village compared with most villages in the Tithandizane area. There is perhaps a little more prosperity and less apathy. In the surrounding fields the crops grow more fruitfully, the land is more fertile. It is quite a different area geographically to the one in which we work. Yet they are not spared when the famine begins to bite. They also grow thinner and hungrier. There too people die.

On my first visit Ndwali takes me round many of the houses, meeting the people of his home village, his childhood companions. He takes me further afield to visit his younger sister who lives in the village of her husband. I had met Sarah soon after my arrival and felt the energy and vivacity that is so similar to my daughter's. She did not stop talking! Once again she chatters on as she shows me her room in her husband's house.

But there is anger too as she points out the room belonging to his new wife. She is angry because two wives should never sleep under the same roof. The marriage is strained by her inability to conceive and she is on a desperate search for a remedy. I feel sad that such a beautiful young woman has been consigned to the restraint of marriage so young.

Ndwali also takes me to meet another beautiful family member - his Ambuya, the grandmother with whom he had spent many of his turbulent teenage years. She occupies a special place in his heart.

She is still working in her field when we arrive, but soon summons some of her extended family to make food for us. Her tall figure is bent with age. However she is still sprightly and her eyes are piercing as she studies me.

Outside on her veranda we offer her the gifts we have brought including massage creams to aid her arthritis. Proudly she shows me her identity card that displays her date of birth. Her appetite for life and interest in the world belies her ninety-five years. Sitting at her feet I grow to love this kindly woman. Like Ndwali I hope that one day she will stay with us in Tithandizane and visit the village of her youth.

One day I also visit some of Ndwali's family in Chipata. We go to collect Mr Ndaka from the house of his brother in the centre of town. There I meet some of the young people in his family, and particularly talk with a couple of the teenagers, comparing life in Britain with life in Zambia. These are beautiful bright young people, facing many hardships but also experiencing the joys of a warm extended family. We talk and talk until finally we become aware of the others waiting in the vehicle to make the journey home. We hope it will not be long till we meet again and continue this conversation.

We will meet, all too soon.

The news comes like a thunderbolt, out of the blue. The next morning we are all ready to go to town, when Ndwali's cousin arrives. One of the beautiful young people I met the previous day is dead. Sudden accidental death.

Rosie was only twenty-four, just a year older than my daughter. She had been gently there in the background as the teenagers and I had our discussions outside the house the previous day. Within hours of our leaving, she fell down a storm drain full of water from the recent rains, and drowned.

Instead of going into town, we go in a different direction to locate Mr Ndaka, the head of the family, tell him the sad news and collect all who are able to travel, to take them to Chipata for the funeral. When we arrive they are out in the fields planting peanuts. It takes a while to find them, and then we wait while they get dressed in their funeral clothes. They reel from the shock of this unexpected death.

We then struggle through unfamiliar bush roads to Chipata. What had once been dry dusty tracks are fast flowing streams, full of the newly arrived torrential rains. Several times we are in danger of getting stuck, some of the men even have to walk in front of us to guide our passage, sometimes we have to leave the "road" and negotiate our way through the bushes that line the narrow foot track beside the "road".

When we finally arrive, the house is sadly different from the previous day. I sit with the women in the house and sing hymns, beautiful in their native tongue. I notice once again the different headscarves on the women and realise that they denote choirs from the different denominations grieving here together, their voices harmonising the hymns to their God. Although I cannot understand the words, I can feel the haunting emotion of the hymns and join in as best I can, pronouncing unfamiliar words sometimes to familiar tunes as I share a hymnbook. We sing together, joining this mother, crying for her loss and remembering our own.

The men go out to collect the firewood for a large fire that will keep them warm outside the house through the night. They also struggle to set up an awning to protect them from the rains; sheets of plastic are tied to the house and to giant logs; this will shelter them in their vigil outside, while the women lay inside on the bare rush mats.

The teenagers now sit at the side of the house weaving beautiful little wreaths and posies made out of paper tissue flowers. For tonight we leave, but tomorrow, once again, I am to be the driver of the hearse.

Early in the morning we return, Ndwali joins the men outside, while I sit with the women inside. We sit for long hours, singing hymns while the family arrives. So many are there that later I am able to follow beckoning from Ndwali's sister and go into the garden, where the silence can softly be broken. We embrace, and exchange a few words, glad to meet again although sad at the circumstances.

Eventually we start out on the long slow journey to the hospital mortuary, the back road that I now know so well. I know all the ruts, the houses beside it, the stall selling this and that as I turn the corner, and the driveway to the mortuary back door around the solitary tree. This time, while some of the women dressRosie's body, I sit on the concrete floor of the waiting room with the family. There is another funeral party there too. We join them as they wait for their loved one's body to be released.

I hear that in a Lusaka hospital there is a death every eight minutes.

Eventually the family files out and surrounds the coffin as it is lowered into the back of our vehicle. Around the coffin the choir sing sweet hymns of sorrow. Behind me Rosie's grieving mother cries as I drive slowly to the church.

It is a large church, painted white with a few simple decorations. It is full of light and in it is held a touching service with many hymns and songs of praise. There are several speakers who tell about this lovely young girl, who despite being hampered by her epilepsy, had done much for the community. It is a long service, made even longer by the large numbers of people crowded into the church who line up to walk around her coffin where she lies in the bloom of her youth.

Rosie looks beautiful. Her dark skin shines against the white satin and lace that lines her coffin.

The mourners circumambulate the coffin gazing at her for the last time, their lips moving in silent prayer. Then we leave the coolness of the church to re-encounter the heat of the sun.

Dark clouds loom on the horizon, though.

Then, there is another slow drive through the beaten earth "streets". It is a difficult drive as we negotiate deep ruts gouged by waters from the rains of many years, now filled with running water from this years' new offerings. Today our vehicle, in my inexperienced hands, can just about manoeuvre them. Soon some will be impassable if the rain continues to fall. The skies threaten, but hold off as we sit in scorching sun in the graveyard. Rosie's Ambuya calls me over from the shadeless spot I have settled on. We share the shade of a small bush as we listen to the pastor's words.

I take in the harsh reality of the cemetery. Line upon line of newly dug graves, some full, some empty. In front of me as I sit, like all the others on the bare earth, is a numbered grave— 412/98. So many graves dug, in one small town, in one cemetery, in one year. It is not a large town. Most who die in the hospital are returned to their home villages to take their final rest. And this is not the only cemetery.

Again there is a long ritual by the graveside; though this is a town funeral in a cemetery, this is not like a western funeral. There is no cleanly hidden, hygienised, and sometimes dehumanised, apology of a ritual here.

Here the reality of life and death is appreciated in full. We all sing and listen and share in the grief. We all take part; each of us picks up a twig, which we give to one of the family when he or she comes to collect it. Then they are counted and together interred with the body. This part of the ritual over, the men, who sit at one side of the grave, take turns to put spadefuls of earth onto the coffin. Finally the young people give out their circlets, sprays and posies, as one by one we are called to lay them on the grave until it is covered with multicoloured tissue flowers.

We return to sit again in the funeral house. It is not quite so solemn here now. Small groups us are called, in turn, to the back room to eat. Funerals are expensive, because all who come must be catered for, for as long as the funeral continues. There is no fancy meal, just the usual nchima, and for me, the vegetarian, beans rather than meat from the specially slaughtered goat.

The house is not so silent now.

I return to the outer room and Rosie's Ambuya calls me over. Mrs Ndaka must have been talking about me! At the graveside Ambuya had indicated her knees as she struggled to rise. Here she does so again. My hands are in demand and fortunately I never travel without my creams and oils. I had not really expected to use them at the funeral, though! We share some deep laughter as I massage her knees. She lifts her skirt a little higher to display the tattooing that men find very erotic. With the assistance of Ndwali's sister she shares this secret of how Ngoni women attract, and keep their men. She asks if I have tattoos.

"No !", I answer, somewhat embarrassed.

She then sticks her tongue out, and graphically makes great fun of our western custom of kissing.

Before darkness falls we depart to carry Mr Ndaka and some of the mourners back to their village. There I am introduced to more of the customs and ritualised form of grieving that is still prevalent in this corner of Zambia. We visit other houses and cry and sit in silence, speak and sing hymns together, to mourn the community's loss.

In future visits I will become more aware of the family conferences that deal with the practical aspects of the aftermath of loss, as well as the complex negotiations that go on between families as part of the process of courtship and marriage. I am privileged to attend one family conference where it is being decided where a widow should live after her husband's death, where her children should go and what the responsibilities of the families involved should be. At other times I learn more about the negotiations that go on between families before a betrothal can be announced.

One day, we again tackle the dirt roads that had become rivers of mud. We have to deliver some food to Ndwali's home village. The famine is biting. We go to visit Ndwali's Ambuya who had been sick. To his delight he is able to persuade her to come back with us to stay for a little while and revisit her birthplace.

Ndwali and Amrita take her on many visits, including into town and to see the newly opened "Shoprite" store. The epitome of consumerism, it is a source of wonder to those villagers who manage to get into town. A variety of goods are under one roof;

previously they had had to search the small "Indian shops" (members of the Indian communities own most of the shops in town) for their necessities, and the colourful market stalls for their fresh food and second hand clothing. Ambuya returns exhausted and astounded.

It is a wonderful visit. I cannot believe that she is ninety-five, and still so sprightly. As Amrita is needed elsewhere I have the huge honour of driving her and Ndwali to her birthplace. Apart from visiting it briefly for her mother's funeral she has not returned for fifty years. It is a neat village, just a little bit off the road midway between Tithandizane and Chipata. As we drive in we are looked at a little curiously, but no one rushes to the vehicle as they do in our own area.

Ndwali goes into one of the huts and returns with a woman who looks rather bemused as she approaches the vehicle. Then I see her spot Ambuya. Her face brightens, and she sends children ahead to tell others of our arrival. As we walk slowly into the village, all attention is focused on Ambuya; we are called into one of the huts where a couple of women are waiting, then more join us and we sit in a circle on the floor. The old women talk together while Ndwali answers the few questions they flash at us.

Apart from at funerals, and the occasional outbursts of anger, this is the most emotion I have ever seen expressed in Zambia. No words, just in tears that trickle down their cheeks. Ndwali later expresses to me, that, at that point, he wondered if he had done the wrong thing in persuading Ambuya to visit her birthplace.

I have a wonderful photo of these old ladies. Beside Ambuya stands a slender elderly woman. She is very upright, not even needing a stick. This is the Aunt who had helped bring Ambuya up. She must be at least one hundred and three years old.

The longevity of the elderly stands in stark contrast with the ever-falling life expectancy in Zambia. With the advent of AIDS, life expectancy is now a mere thirty-eight years.

Life here, for me, is such a bittersweet experience. The generosity and the welcome I find here touches my heart. But, as my friendships grow, I also know how tenuous a hold on life many of my new friends have. England now feels like another world to me.

I pray the world of consumerism will not take such a hold here, while at the same time I wish I could do more to help ease the suffering. I feel small, inadequate and in a way ashamed. I feel the weight of greed and ignorance that has made me blind to how the world is for many people. Particularly I am ignorant about the history of our colonial days that has blighted a lot of families' lives. I am angry about the greed of the banks and corporations that bleed away money that should be spent on health care. Furious with the drug companies that refuse to offer medicines where they are needed.

But, for now, this is a time for putting aside the depression, sadness and fear. This small space of time is given over to the pleasure of spending days with a lady who has much to share.

I chat with Ambuya as we sit preparing vegetables on the step in the hot sun. Ambuya is showing me how to strip the coarse bitter veins off pumpkin leaves so that we can make a tasty relish. Her lively mind darts questions at me as we work preparing a meal for her grandson's return. In the evenings we draw inside the house sheltering from the mosquitoes and sometimes the rain that thunders onto the corrugated iron and off the roof to form a mini lake. Sometimes the sound of the rain drowns our voices. At other times I enjoy sitting silent, massaging her arthritic knees in the light of the kerosene lamp.

When Ndwali joins us I listen to the two of them reminiscing as we stretch out on the floor. I share the joy of watching them glow as they talk together. I am deeply touched to see how this grandmother and grandson obviously adore each other.

CHAPTER ELEVEN

The Man with No Name

I have been here just two months and in some ways it feels like no time at all, and in others it feels like a lifetime. Especially in the depths of some of the friendships I have made. For the first time tonight I cry and cry. Perhaps they are other's tears, not mine, perhaps it is just that they are ours.

Sitting outside perched on a log, no place to hide here, I just want to curl up in a ball and hide from the pai n- the shared pain with the man who is here today. I don't even know his name, but in those few hours we know each other. I doubt I will ever see him again, he lives a fair way out of our area. But his face, his eyes, his hands, his frame are etched on me, the feel of his hands holding mine so tightly, till the moment his ox-cart lurches away. His whispered words, his dignity, and that we offered him. We meet so deeply it hurts. He and I meet in knowing the seriousness of his illness, his family too, but wordlessly denying it holding back in their pain. We shared looks, enough to convey sympathy and understanding. And so I cry at his/their pain, and that it is shared by so many others and at the ignorance of the rest of the world (it seems). And there I catch myself judging…judging is not the answer, who knows what lies behind each person's ways.

This is a turning point for me, in my stay in Zambia, in my understanding of others, and particularly of myself. It has repercussions; on my temper and my health. It opens me out, raw and naked. I see my little self and know more about what I am capable of, for good or for ill. Through that I am more able to understand others even when I am angry with them for their apathy and neglect.

It is just before Christmas, and I am tired. After nearly a year of struggling it looks as if some of the longer-term plans for the project might come to fruition, as they have had good news about grants. The Tithandizane AGM has been an inspiring event. Mike is in great spirits. He has managed to reclaim his children and taken them home to his mother. He is fitter than he has been for a long time, and even working a little. However, what I saw yesterday has saddened me.

I am going to visit Joshua regularly and each visit rips me to bits as I contemplate his suffering in the late stages of AIDS. His quivering hands are ready to push me away in his agony as I clean and redress his suppurating wounds. I feel for his indignity, as he lies on the piece of sacking on the earth floor alone in his hut, totally at the mercy of others.

I also call in to see Paula, who has become a good friend; she also has AIDS and she too looks as if she is deteriorating badly. We sat on her step, long and late last night talking. She reminisces and wonders what the future will hold, looking deeply into her deepest fears.

It is Sunday morning; the clinic is closed, so it is relatively quiet. A few people have come to Tithandizane for books and condoms and I join them in our room beside the clinic. While they look at the books, I sit, in between giving out condoms, on the sacks of sunflower seeds that are waiting to be planted. I hope to get time to read some letters and the Amida newsletter that arrived yesterday. It has a piece about the work of Tithandizane; quotes from my letters are in it too, and it feels strange seeing them in print and being part of *"Amida Trust at Work"*. Dharmavidya and Prasada feel a long way away; it is lovely but bittersweet to get news from home.

Dimly I hear the roll of ox-cart wheels coming up to the centre. My heart sinks. The sound of an ox-cart is always ominous, it usually heralds the arrival of someone who is very sick. The last few days have been tough, I have seen many very sick people, and I feel in need of some respite; just a small piece of time away from this world of suffering. I hear Ndwali's low voice asking questions. The voices come nearer, and a family comes in carrying a man.

I watch as they lay him on the floor weakly groaning. He is almost comatose. I see the other occupants of the room look and avert their eyes. They cannot stand to look. I can almost hear the thoughts going through their heads; they are going through mine. "Not another, this man must surely have AIDS."

He is thin, emaciated; his clothes hang off him as he curls up in a foetal position in the middle of the floor shutting all out. Or trying to, Ndwali tries to ask questions

"What is your name?"

He does not answer.

"Where do you come from?"

No reply.

"How long have you been sick?"

Nothing.

His family try to answer for him. Ndwali and I cannot believe his family that this man has just been like this for two days.

Ndwali tries again to speak with the man, and this time gets a mumbled, incoherent response. Ndwali looks at me, shrugging his shoulders, indicating that I should wait. His face betrays a little of the exasperation he feels at the obvious denial of the man's condition. Then he heads off to try to find the nurse leaving me to sit with the man and his family.

What feels like a long time passes; the other occupants of the room leave or stay, eyes averted. I guess some of them fear that this is the path they may tread. I saw the same looks of guarded fear when we were here with Mike a few weeks previously. I ponder on the morning. Earlier one of the young men in the room had come looking for ointment for herpes, one of the favourite opportunist infections that flare up in an immune deficient body, often signifying the presence of the AIDS virus. He is one of many I fear may be harbouring the virus.

I feel a huge temptation to also avert my eyes. I want to sit and read and ignore the form lying on the floor and his silent, worried family. They alternately stand or pace as they wait. They are also shutting off from the pain they feel, I can see it in their eyes. They are silent, just waiting, perhaps for his death.

I am not proud of how I felt that morning.

Fortunately I did not stay sitting separate. I let the temptation to shut off go past, then reluctantly put aside my precious letters. I got off the pile of sunflower seeds I was perched on, and sat on the floor beside the man in the middle of the room.

I take his hand between my two hands and sit in silence with him for a while. I put my hand on his shoulder sit alongside him for a while. Then I gently rub his shoulder and back. He seems comatose, does not respond.

"What else can I do?"

No one is communicating here. I look at his family, and see their worry. I do not know whether the patient or his family can speak English, but I speak a little anyway. I try some words of reassurance to try to help them cope with their fear. No response.

A tableaux of silent figures surround this man curled up in the middle of the floor.

There is no dignity lying on the floor like this. I feel ashamed that this is all we can offer him. There is a bed in the corner, but it is without a mattress and covered in boxes and books. I continue to hold his hand. I start to feel angry with the family who have dumped him there. Then I remember that I wanted to ignore him too.

Eventually Ndwali returns with the nurse, and the man is lifted onto the mattressless bed that is now cleared and covered with a rush mat. A drip is set up, and life-giving water enters him. Again I am left with him to watch and wait.

He is too sick to even be taken to hospital. I hurt inside as I watch him fight for life. I watch each breath in case he stops breathing. Part of me wishes I wasn't there. Once again the temptation is to draw away, let others do the work. Thoughts tumble around in my head

"I have had enough."

"I am not fit and I can do nothing."

" He cannot see me, why bother to hold his hand?"

" His family should care for him."

Such thoughts, judgements, negativities and temptations rattle around in my head. I get to know these thoughts well. And in this crucible I start to understand more how and why this family are shutting off. I can understand better the roots of the downheartedness that afflict the people here.

I sit with him, mostly silent, but sometimes sharing a few encouraging words. I hold his hand and rub his shoulder. His family also watch him. From time to time, they look at the posters on the walls, and at

Amrita's lovingly drawn map of the area, showing all the villages. They look at the photograph display showing all the activities and facilities now available at Tithandizane and at photos of the work of the villagers getting the materials in, ready to start building.

I try speaking again to the man as he lies there. I speak gently and quietly, words of support and encouragement, as he lies so silent and still. It does not matter that he probably cannot understand; I just want him not to feel so alone. What matters too is that his family can draw some strength from seeing this, and maybe do the same. They start to speak with him. I feel the cloud of despair lifting a little from me as they take more part and interact more with him. They are no longer so completely shut off.

The saline drip is working, I hear murmuring as the man speaks softly to his brother.

"He feels a bit better", he reports.

I remember Mike lying there some weeks before, also close to death. Water, the miracle cure, I had never realised the importance of water until I came to Zambia, and found that what we take for granted in Britain is a precious commodity here. The life giving water steadily drips into this man's vein and he regains consciousness more fully. The drip is removed and he lies recovering a little strength before his journey home. There is nothing more anyone can do for him; however the rain has started and might last for hours so it may be a long wait.

Then the pains catch him, racking his body. He mutters to his brother,

"Diarrhoea."

His brother takes him out in the rain to the latrine; which is tucked away a short walk behind the buildings. I wait, and wait and wait for his return. A half-hour has passed; they have been gone too long. It is still pouring down. The latrine has no roof. He will be soaked. Again I leave my seat, reluctantly, and I head out into the rain, putting on my jacket. His brother is at the entrance to the latrine, the man leans, exhausted, just inside.

"It's too far". He breathes.

The usual two-minute walk is a marathon for him. He is shivering with cold so we have to encourage him to try to make the journey back. His brother goes to one side, I go to his other, then I put my jacket over his thin frame. He rests a slender hand on my shoulder, and we start the long walk back. Two steps, then he sits on his haunches to rest, I squat down beside him as he pants to regain his breath...two steps.... Then another rest...and another, till finally we make it back to the room. He collapses exhausted and shivering onto the bed.

I start rubbing warmth back into his body, rubbing and rubbing, his arms, his shoulders, his back; his brother gets the idea and joins in. Finally the shivering subsides. But I am concerned, he is cold, and he has a long journey ahead of him. He holds my hand tight. I try to explain that I must leave him for a few minutes. Reluctantly he lets it go. I go over to our house to find my spare jumper and socks and bring them back to put them on him. The jumper fitted me quite neatly; it hangs loose on his tall thin body!

He again holds my hand tight, speaking a little now, in English. He is an educated man, and now is interested in what is happening in the project. I don't know what he did for a living, or even exactly where he comes from, only that he is from a village far away, outside our area. They had heard that here at Tithandizane there is some hope of help.

So little hope and so little help, and yet, for now it is enough. Death will come, but perhaps a little more kindly and with more dignity. And with a family who are no longer so shut off and unable to demonstrate their care. He looks deeply into my eyes, for a long time. He holds my hand tightly as we wait until the rains abate and it is time to go. He looks deeply into my eyes, with a look that goes to my heart, and holds my hand as they lift him into the ox cart, holds it until the very last moment when the cart starts rumbling away.

We met in the centre of his pain. Helper and helped become one.

This was a big learning for me, seeing the judgmental part of me, and letting go of the judgement of others. I am more able now to see how I can turn away. I can see my own frailty, know it and forgive myself for it. In forgiving myself, I can forgive others. Not only that, it has the potential of helping me see when I need to do the helping, whether it is my need, or the others' need. And to see when it is time to let others to do the helping. Often there is no more to do than show others the way. Often there is no more to do than to love each other.

CHAPTER TWELVE

Christmas in No Man's Land; New Year with the Nyou

It is mostly smaller things that bring it home to me that I am in Africa. Most of the time I am just involved with people. It does not matter that we speak different languages, have different customs, and look so different. There is a real sense of community as they laugh at my feeble actions and speech and help me learn. There is much commonality, in hopes and dreams and fears, and humanity. It is almost more accessible here. I start to see how much family and community feeling we have lost in the West

Sometimes I see a wider view, often literally. I notice the moon in this southern sky, or as I did earlier as I drove to the village, I saw the panorama of the African bush laid out before me. Flat land, sparsely vegetated with trees. Islands of amazingly shaped stone-cropped hills against it, in the distance, dark and looming, while above is a brilliant azure sky. This time of the early rains is so different from my first month or so of heat-hazed dusty landscapes.

It is Christmas Eve, early afternoon. Amrita arrives to collect me from my marathon stint of baking with the MP's children; all her last minute visits are complete and now we are going to Malawi. Ndwali is away back to his home village, so the house is empty. Tom our neighbour and enthusiastic helper, a young man crippled by polio but bursting with the energy of life accompanies us. He is keen to get a trip into new territory, and he can help push or find local assistance if the vehicle breaks down (as it does frequently).

En route we pick up James, Esther and Gotami's, brother. This is to be a Christmas with Gotami's family, time for her to see the father she has not seen for quite a while. I am shocked when I meet James. He is fourteen-years old, but smaller than Gotami, who is nine. I wonder if I have heard is age wrongly. No. When their mother died he remained with relatives while Gotami was adopted by Amrita.. The effects of the ensuing difference in diet over the last few years shows dramatically. In his home, with distant relatives, he lives a very hard life spending much of his time as a street vendor, selling maize fritters and cakes.

I fall in love immediately with James. His beaming mischievous smile, and willingness to join in with whatever is happening with wonderful good humour, brightens our days. His resilience is amazing.

It is lovely going away with these children. I am, however, also feeling quite some trepidation. This is my first time going over a land border into another country and I am nervous of the customs post. Also the policemen, who stride around with rifles slung over their shoulders scare me. Though, in fact, our contacts with police have been very friendly and often we give them lifts on our visits to town. They were kind when I had my purse stolen, doing their utmost to recover it and bring the culprits to trial.

My fears are groundless; crossing the border proves no problem at all. Now we are in "No man's land" the area just over the Malawi border, where Gotami's father lives. There is a desolate feel to the area around the border. Even though the tarmac road cuts a way through it, it feels isolated from the rest of the world. Mostly there are few trees or dwelling places.

It looks grey. It echoes my own humour as I face my first Christmas away from my children and family and friends. Loneliness is biting me even though I am among good friends. The realities of the life here feel overwhelming - the hunger and pain and suffering I witness and can do so little about.

I am also worried about the weather; I do not like the look of the looming iron-grey clouds and I am right to be wary. Tropical rainstorms are nothing compared with even the worst tempests in Britain. As we draw off the tarmac onto the dirt road leading to the village the heavens open. Sheets of water fall from the sky. They drum on the roof, deafening us and making conversation impossible. Within minutes, inches of water lie on the ground and soon there is a foot-deep flood and the sandy soil turns to a thick slippery sea of mud. Soon all we can see is a sea of mud before us.

The distinction between road and field is lost and we see-saw from side to side as Amrita tries to keep the vehicle on the road. Failure. The vehicle grinds to a halt as the engine revs are lost.

My heart sinks — I suspect this mud has similar characteristics to the snow I battled with in the mountains of Scotland, and will be even more unforgiving. Women and children pile out into the meagre shelter of banana trees. They are all laughing as if this is the best entertainment. They cheer on the men who dig away the mud and put stones under the wheels

– men who appeared as if from nowhere to come to our aid.

But I am still grumpy, missing my children terribly and, I am sorry to say, not joining in their good humour. In fact I am in a very bad humour - most of all with the driver. Poor Amrita got rather fed up with me that day I think! . In "No Man's Land" we get stuck in the mud twice and have to get out into this rain to try to get the vehicle out. It looks impossible; however with much pushing, mud flying we get going again.

We finally arrive at Gotami's father's village. To his astonishment, he was not expecting a visit at all. All the family and the community are delighted to see Amrita; she has a special place in their hearts. They are touched by the care she takes of Gotami and amazed at the amount Gotami has grown while in her care. They are kind and welcoming to us all, finding a room for us to sleep in. Then immediately put on the pots for a meal.

In this land of so little food the biggest gift they can give is a meal and they give again and again. The people here, scrub out a subsistence living from the poor soil and have to travel a long way into Malawi for services. They speak the same language as many in Zambia – Chinyana - but somewhat differently as it is nearer to pure Chewa. The men eat together in another small house, the Insaka, served by the women. I observe that people here do not speak nearly so much, or laugh as much as people in Zambia. They ask relatively few questions, their whole demeanour is more reticent and low key than that of most of the Zambians I have come to know.

The village is clean and neat, without the noise and rowdiness I am now accustomed to. It feels strange. I later learn that part of the reserve is probably due their different political history in Malawi. Malawi had been a very repressed society under the Banda regime, which existed until eight years previously. They had to adhere to very rigorous rules, and so developed a great caution in speech. A caution that still remains.

Christmas is barely acknowledged here. It is work in the fields as usual. However there is one great gift. Christmas morning I have a surprise. We are offered a bath, in a wonderful tin bath full of steaming water. Not just a bath, but to be bathed, as is the tradition here, by their Ambuya. Wonderfully refreshed, we make visits around the whole village, delivering presents of razor blades and soap, while Amrita gives them all the latest news from Zambia.

Amrita, on one of her visits, made great improvements to their well, which has helped reduce their health problems hugely. Proudly they take us to the well to show that it is still in good order.

Then after a lunch of the usual nchima with a relish made from rape, a kind of cabbage we then go visiting further afield before returning to Zambia. En route we look up an old acquaintance of Amrita, and there we receive the best Christmas gift of all, avocado leaves with which to make a healing drink rich in iron to stop anaemia, and the promise of avocado trees once the Tithandizane land is delineated.

The old year dies in scenes that are etched on my memory. Amrita wants to show me dancing in the Chewa tradition. The Nyau. I have seen her dance with the Ngoni, seen their style of dancing with its shouts and foot stamping and acrobatics. Now she wants me to see another world of dance. The drums beckon. We can hear them throbbing in the distance. The passing of one year into the next is a traditional time to dance.

Amrita, Esther and I go hunting the drums. We get lost, get nearly stuck in the mud, get frustrated almost to the point of giving up, tempers are frayed, we are tired. I am missing my family, they seem a long way away, we nearly give up, just have one last try, and then we strike gold.

There in Nkuta, at a village far off the road we find the Nyau. We follow the sound of the drums, an insistent heartbeat that beckons us into the heart of the village. In a large cleared area we see a circle of women and children, shapes in the moonlight clapping and swaying. The men loll around on the outskirts of the dancing, and we see them being shooed a greater distance away; men, other than the dancers are not allowed to watch. It is a secret society, inspired by the power of the dance only open to those men daring enough to go into its embrace.

It is nearly midnight, the circle of women surround the performers as they act out scenes of stories in a rhythmic and acrobatic, fast swirling dance. They play animals that are so life like you can almost believe in them. It is a form of entrancement. Together with rest of the women I sashay to the rhythm, they encourage me to join in; our bodies connect as we sway and call and hoot to encourage the dancers ever onwards in their story of life. One after the other the dancers take the stage, leaping into the arena and battling for possession. It is a magical experience, mystical, the old year ends on a wondrous note, the new year enters wrapped in mystery.

CHAPTER THIRTEEN

In Sickness and in Health

"Oh how sick I am of mud and mosquitoes and smelly latrines, and cold bowl washes and the ever present malaria. But oh how I feel for these people, these friends. So many and so different, yet each one and I are just the same. It is beyond colour, black or white. It is beyond being rich or being poor, healthy or unhealthy. We are just in this life together. And in learning together here today I see hope for a better future...I seem to belong to so many different communities in this world now. So diverse, and yet so similar in our shared humanity. Friendship transcends all boundaries."

New Year's day. We come down to earth with a bang. The nurse is sick so we have to help at the clinic; she has malaria. Malaria is a killer, it accounts for thirty percent of health centre and hospital admissions and according to recent reports the fatality rate has more than quadrupled. Adults have some immunity, developed from repeated attacks. Seeing the babies with it turns the knife in me. Often in the middle of the night desperate parents, their children having fits from the fevers, or, the worst, from cerebral malaria, wake us.

I will never forget one young pregnant woman. I first saw her lying in a bed in the bare clinic room.

We hear that she is fitting interminably; chloroquine has not worked, nor quinine tablets. Now she is on a quinine drip, a horrible and dangerous treatment and needs urgently to get to hospital. A tropical rainstorm is upon us, the road is impassable; all we can do is wait and hope that the rain will stop in time for us to take her to hospital.

Meanwhile we try to offer some comfort to her and her family. She lies on the bed in the gloomy light, her body convulsing every few minutes, her face drawn up into a grimace and her eyes rolling in her head, vacant and unaware of anything apart from the fear these convulsions engender. Her young husband lies with his head on her belly, weeping; at the foot of the bed her young child cries for his mother's breast while his grandmother rocks him in her arms trying to comfort him. We are powerless to do more; all I can do is hold the young woman's hand and wait. We wait for death, or for the rains to stop so the vehicle can get her to hospital; even then we are doubtful whether she will survive.

She is doubly lucky, the rains stop in time to get her to hospital; and she survives. We had left her in the hospital holding out little hope for her survival and thinking that even if she does she will be permanently severely brain damaged. Weeks pass and we hear how she clings onto life. Then one day when we are collecting patients from the hospital, she is there. The young woman and her beaming family surround us as we help people into the truck. Holding my arm for support she gets inside the truck softly but clearly offering her thanks. Our hearts lifted, we drive her home.

Three days into the New Year, I feel sick, my whole body aches, I have pains in my stomach. I feel like I have a. bladder infection. I blame myself for ignoring symptoms of dehydration. On long journeys into the bush on foot it is difficult to carry enough water, and the previous day had been long and hard, busy from dawn till dusk, and beyond, in the sultry heat. I try to pour liquid into my thirsty body; I have a thirst that cannot be quenched.

As I suffer, I realise how much the people suffer, the pain in the body and especially the head are just transitory for me; for others they are repeated time after time. Most women have to carry on no matter how ill they are, working in the fields and feeding their families. The men are a little more fortunate; they can come in from the fields and lie down.

I try to stop, but I also have to work. There are people to take home from the hospital, and Amrita and Ndwali are busy. At the end of the day when I go to collect Amrita and Ndwali from the MP's house I am feeling very sick indeed. I am frozen cold, shivering and feel terribly nauseous; I ache from head to toe as if I have the worst dose of "flu" imaginable, even worse.

Ndwali now takes a hand, insisting I have to accept that it is malaria and that the prophylactic drugs I hoped would protect me from malaria have not worked. The MP's wives put me in a bath to warm me up and to help ease my aching body before we return to Tithandizane.

Back home I crawl onto my mattress. I feel close to death. Nightmares come and go. The head pain is beyond belief, worse than the worst migraine I have ever encountered, and in the midst of those I had been known to bang my head against the wall, that pain being "better" than the pain of the migraine.

Here, now, I am too weak to even contemplate that. My whole body hurts, every bone, every muscle, every inch of my body seems to be screaming. Every system is affected; the parasite has got out of control and invaded every part of me. Now the chloroquine is trying to kill it off. I can feel the battle within.

Time drags by and I start to recognise the avoidance that has made me deny that I am sick, making matters worse. Then, I am angry, very angry, railing inside at being in this position, weak and in pain. I feel the fear that lies behind the anger, fear of pain and suffering and of death itself; then I realise that I am not just angry or fearful for myself, but also for the people here, angry at all the suffering they undergo. I feel the hopelessness and fear that lie beneath their apparent apathy, their withdrawal from the pain and powerlessness of their lives in the face of so much illness and deprivation.

I understand so much more now.

Then suddenly all the angst drops away. I feel a strange kind of calm. The anger and fear melt and disappear. I still feel the pain, but now as I sweat and toss and turn, inside I am at peace. I will accept whatever comes, I am ready to die; I am also ready to live. I understand now how the people also find so much joy in living and in the world around them. I also feel a joy for living, an appreciation of all that has been. I even feel a touch of excitement. What will dying feel like? What lies next?

I now know I want to die consciously. I know why I have taken this Buddhist path, it offers no answers to what death will bring; it just offers living to the full and dying to the full. I feel full of gratitude to all I have encountered, my parents, my children, my teachers, and my friends. I feel rich in the fullness of life, and live.

Ndwali sees me struggling out to the latrine the following morning. No sweet words come from him:

"I'm glad you have malaria, you will know what it feels like and you will write from experience."

That was harsh, but there was great truth in it. Knowing what it feels like means that I will detect it sooner next time, and take action sooner. Also, writing from experience, and talking from experience, to a Western world that does not understand; might help people to understand the desperate state, healthwise, his people are in.

I grow a lot from that experience. I have faced one of my greatest fears, and have not crumbled when facing it. I have also touched the joy that lies even within suffering; but above all I now truly understand how his people are suffering. I am one of them. And I receive the great gift of knowing that death itself is not something to be afraid of. Though I must admit, for me, the process leading up to it is scary.

There are a large number of people around the following morning, waiting to go in the vehicle to Chipata. They watch as I go back and forth to the latrine to vomit and release the diarrhoea. They watch as I go to get cup after cup of water. They watch me through the open doorway to the communal room as I lie on my bed. They watch as I also, take my medicine.

I feel them studying my reactions, and hear their sympathetic laughter. I am a fellow patient like them. They watch me survive, and they watch me stay. I do not run away. I feel their friendship. Malaria is part of everyone's lives here, and I am now, even more, part of their lives too.

I am now not the only one sick, I had prayed that the others would not get it, but little Naomi is burning and crying. I know how she feels. I fear for her, her already tiny frame seems too delicate to take such a horrible illness. Within hours that lively little girl has become tearful and lethargic and burning hot to touch.

Malaria affects everyone differently. With the form of malaria prevalent here in Zambia, the symptoms vary, so everyone has to be extra vigilant. I am in some ways fortunate, I never get the extremes of vomiting I see in Amrita, Gotami and Ndwali. We all get it again and again it goes round in circles, for the rest of the duration of my stay, and beyond.

I think of other friends we have recently taken to hospital, who are sick and fighting for their lives. I speak with Ndwali one night soon afterwards, as we wait outside the hospital, having delivered a close friend who is very sick and fighting for his life. I realise that here in Zambia there is no respite from illness. Again and again we all face sickness and death.

"The only respite is to laugh and enjoy to the full all the good things life can offer." Is Ndwali's response.

I sit on the step outside the hospital, I look at the stars above, and at the hazy moon that peeps out between the dark clouds. I feel the presence of Quan Shi Yin, the bodhisattva of compassion, and feel the quiet tears in me. Bodhisattvas are seen in Buddhist iconography as wisdom beings that can guide and help us. They can be mythological, or seen as archetypes, or seen as an aspect of every person we meet. Some people like Mother Theresa can also be seen as living bodhisattvas. We can feel their presence with us helping us face or do whatever is needed. Feeling Quan Shi Yin's helpful presence helps me be open to my friends' pain, and to my own. She helps me see all people and circumstances as my friends; and now I can see that, in a crazy way, the malaria has also been my friend too.

We are lucky, thanks to Amrita's persistence and persuasion to have a short break from work. We plan a trip to a wildlife reserve where she has friends who will put us up.

It is a long drive to the Mfui Wildlife Park. A dozen of us are crammed into the truck along with mattresses, bedding etc. I join some of the kids in the open back, sheltering from the rain under a tarpaulin; we are full of laughter as we hide from the rain, trying to make sure none of us gets too wet as the water tries to creep in through the many holes. However after that rainy first day, we are scorched from the sun. The rains, already upon us in Kamulaza are late in coming to Mfui.

On the way we stay a night at an empty house at the school where some of Amrita's friends teach. They are already starting to fear that again there will be no crops. Already they have planted their seeds twice. They pray for rain. But for now they put these fears aside and join us on our trip.

What an experience; I feel like a child again, seeing a totally new world. Not only the animals, but also the trees, many are huge and different, and the shapes they form against the sparkling azure skies are spectacular. The birds fill the air with song; we don't always see them, just catch sight of flashes of brilliant colour that dart into the trees. On the ground are strange ungainly guinea fowl with bright blue necks that root around amongst the undergrowth. We see other birds that are large and graceful, the black and white sacred Ibis, marabou storks tall and elegant, and numerous birds totally different from those I am used to seeing in our Western Hemisphere.

Seeing the animals in their natural surroundings is stunning. Many years ago I had been sickened by the plight of some animals in zoos, and have never been to a wildlife centre since, so memories of seeing wild animals are very dim, and somewhat disturbing.

It is magical. I never expected to see elephants and giraffes and zebras and warthogs here in Zambia. Today it is like seeing them in glorious Technicolor. We are all excited, even those who have been before. We stand up in the slow moving vehicle, balancing precariously and calling to each other, pointing out our sightings. Inside the vehicle Esther, Naomi, Gotami and the others who hide there from the heat of the sun, lean out of the windows, craning their necks to see as much as possible.

We get close to several families of elephants, they are huge, yet beautifully proportioned and dark, dark, grey against the green foliage; their ears are like gigantic fans, sweeping gracefully backwards and forwards. There are whole families, from the huge wrinkled elderly elephants, to babies scampering at their mother's heels. A large old tusker moves onto the road and starts to stride towards us, then stops as we stop. He stands guard, we have to stop and watch and wait as his family crosses the road; a long line of them. He waits carefully watching us to make sure we do no harm, until the last little one has safely crossed the road, then they slowly move away, melting into the bush.

Many times I feel that we are being studied, just as we study them. We see the zebras; they are much larger than I expect them to be. They look like large horses, striped black and white; they stand in small groups, families of them watching us warily, yet not too frightened of these intrusive strangers. They even seem inquisitive.

We see troupes of baboons in the undergrowth and around the dried up riverbed. Then we see the giraffes, they are even taller than I imagined, their long legs and long necks, move in tandem as they stride around, from time to time stretching to reach high branches, their heads are surprisingly small and their faces gentle.

I can't stop laughing at the warthogs. At first glance they just look like hairy pigs until they look full at us, and their comical features can be seen. They survey us, but at first sight of a camera, or so it seems, they dart off into the undergrowth.

It is a glorious day, full of joy and laughter and sights I never believed I would be gifted to see.

CHAPTER FOURTEEN

Paula's Story

Amidst all these hard things I see and feel I realise so much the importance of finding the joys in life. And there are many, often such simple things. Fireflies dancing as we stop to let off passengers on the journey home. A gift of a plate of honey, the first in two months. Laughter as the women dance in a village en route – I am very tempted to join in! And every night an amazing light show, as the lightening illuminates the skies.

I meet Paula the day I arrive, before we even go to our house. She and her husband had become close friends of Amrita. In fact the day I arrived Amrita had been searching for medicine in Lusaka for him. She wants me to meet them urgently because she is very concerned for their health and knows they need much support.

A shock awaits us. Amrita goes into the house and finds that he died from AIDS the day I arrived in Zambia. I go in too, I am not aware that this is an unusual funeral house. After the burial the previous day, his family, who had wanted it over quickly, had abandoned Paula and left her alone.

There is no silence in this funeral house. Paula needs to talk. We hear all about her husband's last days, Amrita had not expected him to die so soon, and the fact that it had happened while she is away is a heavy blow to her too. He had been a very good friend to her; they had both given her much support in the tough early days of the project. She is also very sad that she missed the burial. They grieve together. Mike, Gotami and I watch on sadly in that little house by the road.

Her husbands' family will not allow Paula to stay long in the house. They want nothing more to do with her; they blame her for leaving her first husband and marrying their son. They claim she bewitched him. So Paula has to return to her own village. Her family give her a house on the outskirts of their village, her sister and her young daughter join her.

One morning, early, a young boy on a bicycle is knocking on our door with a message, "Paula is very sick, please come."

We go. She now, on top of the HIV, has malaria to contend with. She is very sick indeed. The vomiting is racking her delicate body; she lies in her bed too weak to move. But despite that, she still has to welcome visitors properly, and sends her sister to make tea. Amrita gives her some ORS to restore the fluid balance, then we sit either side of her in the near dark; the bed only just fits in the room so there is nowhere else to sit. I adjust to the surroundings. It is a very feminine space, brightly coloured chitengis adorn the walls, and coloured blankets are on top of the bed. In a way the space reflects her beauty.

She is very beautiful, tall and elegant with fine features and a smooth skin; occasionally her face and eyes are lit up by a smile; however most of the time her eyelids are lowered as if to shield her eyes from the pain she feels as she speaks about her husband's last days. She talks about the pain, mental and physical she is going through as she mourns her husband and faces the ravages of malaria and AIDS. We can do no more than be with her. The visit though, lifts her a little out of the depths of fear and depression she has sunk into.

A couple of days later I return alone, to see how she is doing. She is feeling a little better and pleased to have a visitor. I join her on the bed, her sister brings tea and she talks about her husband, her love for him, his kindness, and her loneliness. She shines as she speaks about him. Unlike most marriages made in her society it was a love match that took place relatively late in their lives. She had led a colourful life prior to meeting him, with many partners, hence his family's non-acceptance of her. But on meeting him her life changed utterly and they were blissfully happy until he started getting sick.

She is left at the mercy of his family and will probably be left with nothing in the way of possessions and money; however she is relieved to be back with her own family. She misses her husband badly, struggling with the loneliness of no longer having him beside her, physically and emotionally.

The rituals still alive in their society help her. She tells me about some of these rituals that a wife goes through after the husband dies. She proudly shows me a cord that runs round her body, crossed between her breasts, this is tying her to her husband even beyond death. She will not be allowed to remove that cord for a long time. Also, in bed, she is only allowed to sleep in one position, lying on her back, again for a prescribed period of time.

We talk about our families. She is keen to know about mine, and the customs in our society. The next time I return, in the dim light we spend a long time poring over photos of our respective families, exchanging information and bringing them to life. I am thankful that I had brought a small album of photos; they help me be seen as a real person to many people. They can see me as a daughter, sister, wife and mother.

Sharing our photos and our stories bring Paula and I very close, our friendship grows and I start to feel that I have found another sister.

Paula shares her grief and her fears about what will happen to her child when her times of sickness escalate and she draws closer to death. As she talks I put my arm round her shoulders, and she leans against me, I feel how thin she is against my roundness. Her skin is moulded over her cheekbones so that she looks like a piece of beautifully carved sculpture. Her shaven head only makes her more beautiful. Her fingers are long and tapering, they hold mine tight as we talk.

When Amrita and I visit again, Paula is still very ill. Her body aches interminably. She has a sore lump in her stomach that she displays to us, wincing at the slightest touch. She has painful lump in her neck too. She opens her blouse to demonstrate the thinness that frightens her. Her small breasts sag, and every rib is carved out under her skin. She turns over on the bed and lies so that I can gently massage away some of the pain. Her wide shoulders are etched out under my fingertips, under her sleek smooth skin I can see every knob of her backbone. Gently I rub the oil into her smooth skin, not so much a massage as a declaration of affection in human touch, one sister caring for another.

Repeated infections attack her body and she is in constant pain. She comes with us to the hospital, struggling to walk along the long corridors hoping that an ultrasound scan will reveal something that explains the pain and is treatable. It shows up swollen lymph nodes, but nothing else to indicate the source of her pain. The doctor just gives her vitamins for now; perhaps the swollen lymph nodes are evidence of limited defences being marshalled to fight off the repeated infections. But, it could be tuberculosis. As with Mike, a biopsy is suggested, with all its attendant risks. She now has a big decision to make.

I visit often. My visits to the further out villages to give massages frequently take me past her door. She lives a few kilometres from my home and somehow always hears when I am in the vicinity and puts the water on for tea. She knows my vice! She has a large metal mug that she fills to the brim. Our friendship grows. We both need this friendship .she in her pain, and I in my aloneness. We talk deeply, and as our friendship develops we can ask each other the questions no one else will ask.

She is a good friend of Amrita too. Amrita loves Paula dearly too, but the many demands on her time mean she cannot visit all she likes. My visits to Paula also offer me sweet respite. There is joy in our friendship; we share much laughter despite Paula's sickness. She is always as ready to laugh as to release her more painful emotions. Her courage gives me strength as I face my own loneliness.

A couple of weeks before the New Year, fresh pain and diarrhoea and vomiting hit Paula. She is visibly losing even more weight; all the contours of her skull can be seen below the tautly stretched skin. She is getting worse, not better, her will to live is fading, and she feels like giving up. She has sent her daughter away to live with her sister, to ensure that she is properly cared for, and so that her daughter does not witness her decline and death.

We sit on the mud step of her house, darkness has fallen, and the rains are not yet here. It is a warm, soft, tropical night. She shares some of her fears with me, and her feeling of hopelessness. I realise that the need is to get beyond the limitations of speech to the unvoiced fears and superstitions. We sit outside quietly; all I can do is point out the beauty of the evening, as we sit under the thatched eaves, that stand out against a star filled sky. I point out the silhouetted trees, and a new moon that sparkles just above the horizon.

For me this moon is a reminder of Quan Shi Yin, the "hearer of the cries of the world" as she is also known. I hold my pendant in my hand as we talk; it also depicts Quan Shi Yin the bodhisattva who is my comfort and support. I give Paula a little calendar, depicting Quan Shi Yin with her flask of kindness; there is nothing more I can do at this time other than point out the beauties of this world, and share with Paula my vision.

As we sit in companionship and peace, I decide that this is the time to risk a direct question. For her to be able to make a decision I know she needs to give voice to her deepest fears.

I ask bluntly, "What do you fear most?"

Her words tumble out,

"Going the way of my husband. He suffered terribly, I could do nothing, he was so sick, so much pain, could not eat, could not drink, I am scared of the pain, scared of this sickness, scared of the demons at work."

Low voiced with fear she speaks of her husband, his sickness and his death. The way that his mouth and throat furred up with candida so that he could no longer manage to eat and drink, the fever that racked his body, the sweats and the shivering, the vomiting and diarrhoea. His suffering that is now hers.

She speaks of the blame. The blame his family puts on her for bringing death to him. And of her own guilt because she believes she brought AIDS to him.

But above all her fear is of travelling that same road.

Back in Britain, before the triple drug therapy evolved I had heard my friends with HIV speaking of this same fear, when they were left after partners died. This is the cruelty of this illness; it is harder for the one left behind. They know the road before they even tread it.

I have to leave her. I hardly sleep that night, worrying about whether I have done the wisest thing, opening up the wound and leaving her with the poison flowing out. Might that have pushed her over the edge into totally giving up? On the other hand, I also question whether I am right encouraging her to live, extending her suffering. I do not know. A couple of days later as I go back to see her, I am full of apprehension. What will I find?

She sits outside on the step of her house; she looks calm, more resolute. Her decision is made, she will have one more try at life, and if she dies in the operation, that is OK too. She will have the biopsy. On New Year's Eve she enters the hospital. She goes with resignation, a shutting off that I have seen in others close to death. As she goes away with Amrita in the vehicle, I fear that it will be the last time I see my friend.

Two weeks later she re-emerges. She has survived!

She goes from strength to strength as the drugs deal with the TB. She finds a new lease of life. A precarious hold on life, yes. It might not be for long. She is always conscious of that. She will always be open to new infections. Her battered immune system can only take so much. The TB drugs themselves take their toll as the toxic effects build up. But her quality of life improves dramatically. She puts on a little weight, she has a hunger for food, especially rice and fresh vegetables; and a hunger for life.

A photo taken soon after shows her, resplendent in her Sunday best, once again a very beautiful elegant woman. Within weeks she is able to travel about again, in a way I have never seen before. She is desperate to get all she can out of the life she has remaining.

In our previous musings we had dreamt of going into town for tea and cakes. The day arrives. I don't think that cakes have ever tasted better!

She is now getting bored as her mental energy returns, though physically she is still limited. We have come up with a scheme to entertain her, make her a little cash and give me something to take back to Britain that can both raise cash, and awareness. She is also desperate to find something to do that can help others in turn; so, we comb the shops for knitting wool.

We buy wool in the Amida colours, and she starts knitting. From that day onwards she is never seen without her knitting needles. She knits woolly hats, each one a different size and design, all a deep red and ochre, with the words Amida Trust emblazoned on them.

At the end of my stay I leave her still knitting, still enjoying life. And alongside her daughter who has returned to live with her mother. The fear of immediate death has receded.

CHAPTER FIFTEEN

Joshua's Story

The lack of will, the sense of hopelessness, is potentially more disastrous than the actual circumstance. Time and time again we see this. I hurt inside even as I write. I hurt so often. This bodhisattva path is lined with thorns. No easy road to travel, to be truly open to what others feel; so many people hurting so much. It's almost beyond our Western comprehension. My words can hardly do it justice.

I am very glad of the respite that tea with Paula offers me. In her village we are asked to visit a man who is very sick with AIDS. We are shown to a small hut in the middle of the village. We bend low to go through the doorway; there is barely room for Amrita and me to stand. Inside there is only a small table bearing a half-eaten piece of nchima and a cup of water; then we notice a bundle on the floor. The bundle groans and moves. Joshua is lying on a piece of sacking on the hard earth floor, covered with a thin, dirty blanket. There is not even a rush mat.

"What is wrong"? Amrita enquires as she bends down closer to him.

Joshua groans as he pulls the blanket away from his body, and with blackened hands pulls up his filthy trouser to reveal a dirt-grimed leg. He indicates, around his knee, an even dirtier piece of cloth tied in a knot. Amrita squats on the floor beside him and gently takes off the makeshift bandage to reveal a large, encrusted, suppurating sore. Joshua cries out as she cleans the wound. He shivers with pain, shudders at every touch. Otherwise he is silent. Wordlessly he points to other sores.

I feel a burning anger at his neglect. I share this with Amrita as we drive home. We also share our fears about the danger of burn out. For Amrita, this is almost one too many. Recently several friends have died, and others are very sick. This man will need frequent visits to redo dressings and apply ointments, I am fresher, and as he lives quite near and needs no complicated treatment, I undertake to visit Joshua regularly.

We have heard of Joshua too late to do much more than dress his wounds and soothe his pain. We can do little more than this and offer loving care for his last days.

The next time I visit I come with Ndwali. Joshua still lies dirty and uncared for. He is giving up on life on that hard earth floor, on that single piece of sacking. The anger in me wells up again, huge anger that we humans can so neglect a man. Where is his family?

I am no nurse, no expert in dressing the kinds of wounds that he gradually exposes to me. Joshua is little more than a skeleton covered with skin. Skin that because of the pressure of his bones on the earth is oozing with sores. Sores that his nearly defunct immune system cannot hope to heal. The dirt he lies in, the dirt from his filthy blanket and on his own body, make it even worse.

He seems to have only a sole surviving sister and her marital family living nearby; we beg them to help him bathe, they say he will not let them help him, it hurts too much. Ndwali goes back in the evening and manages to help him bathe. Now we can really start to give him the care he badly needs.

I will never forget my first sight of him as he lies on the ground in front of his rickety door, or the first time I have to dress his wounds. I call every few days. I see his sister from time to time, and have difficulty curbing my anger at what I perceive to be continued neglect. Again and again I make pleas for his care. She nods each time and seems to understand but still we find him dirty and unkempt.

We provide vitamins and minerals to boost his immune system and every other day I dress his wounds. His hands are ever ready to push mine away as I gently try to remove the sodden bandages that stick so hard to his tender skin. Every one removed is torture to him, but together we manage. One at a time the sores are cleaned and dressed, and I pad the wounds to give them some protection. Gradually, on each visit he shows me more sores. They cover almost every part of his body; legs, and arms, backbone and hipbone, elbows and knees, but sorest of all are those on the pelvic bones.

On each visit he collapses with exhaustion and relief once treatment is over. For many visits he does not have anything to say. I guess he is nearly mute with pain, and the indignity of it all.

From what I see this indignity is the worst thing for many suffering with AIDS and similar illnesses. This is where I feel that perhaps I can help him most. I try to do everything gently and kindly in a meditative way. I need to be sharply aware of every move I make so that I cause him the least pain. I try to respect his dignity when necessarily he has to reveal his body for the sores to be tended.

He begins to speak to me and to take interest in the world again; both his own world and beyond its borders. He has no hope of recovery and yet he has recovered perhaps what he needed most.

As the weeks pass, Joshua's spirits improve greatly. He can even laugh. More people visit him now and he is actually, with encouragement manages to sit outside his hut. I discover his passion for boiled rice, and sugar. His appetite has returned. He is enjoying life again.

The children in Joshua's village are my quarrelsome friends; they join me and sit arguing on the step as I visit Joshua. They wait for me to dress his wounds, and then present me with theirs. As time goes by, Joshua's condition worsens; the children lift my spirits, just as I try to lift Joshua's. I know him better now and he trusts me to dress his wounds and also likes me to gently rub arnica cream on his painful ribs and back. But there is not an ounce of flesh to protect his bones from the hard ground.

His Indian summer passes. Once again his appetite withers away and the diarrhoea increases. He gets weaker and often his head hurts. I sit cross-legged behind him, then he lies back, his head resting in my lap and I gently massage some of the pain away. I feel a deep tenderness towards him. I am touched by his trust in me and in the midst of his suffering, our shared suffering, there is a kind of peace. I can feel his love.

One night he is even sicker; too sick for me to change his dressings. He hides under his blanket, unable to speak coherently. He is lying on the dirt floor. Only a small piece of sacking lies below his upper body because he is wracked by diarrhoea. He is in danger of rolling into the unguarded wood fire that is close beside him.

I am in a rage at finding him in this state. My young friends go to look for Joseph, Ndwali or anyone who can help. I send other youngsters to find his sister to remake the fire and get an adequate blanket. His sister returns and I struggle to hold back the angry words that threaten to erupt as she tends to the fire. Joshua groans as we roll him onto the sacking and then lies curled up in a foetal position. I caress his head, holding him for as long as can. But as night falls I have to go.

In the night he dies.

There were four deaths that night, three from AIDS.

When I hear, I go to pay my respects to Joshua and his family and sit in vigil with them at his sister's house.

The family call me into inner room, to join them. We sit within touching distance of Joshua's body. Ironically, lying there in his death, wrapped in a blanket, he looks more comfortable than when I was with him the previous night. He has a long thin body. I think of Auschwitz and Bergen Belsen as I look at the form wrapped in a blanket. I remember holding his body, little more than a living skeleton. Already there is a smell of decomposing flesh that lingers in the nostrils.

They have to have the burials quickly for virus-ridden bodies decay quickly in the sultry heat of the rainy season.

As I sit I remember the courage of the man; his gentleness and dignity in the midst of his pain. My hands remember the feeling of holding his head. My heart though filled with sorrow is touched by the gift of trust he bequeathed to me.

He is buried the next day. Again I sit in vigil with the women, then join the procession behind the coffin. Relays of men carry the simple wooden coffin on wooden stretchers to his woodland resting site.

Afterwards the Induna makes a speech, in which, among many other things, he thanks me for all I have done. I am glad when Ndwali takes the stage to say that such help should not be needed and makes an impassioned plea for the community to take more care of their sick members, so that such neglect never occurs again.

I had felt extreme anger and particularly felt it towards Joshua's family. However it is too easy to be judgmental, to point the finger and blame the family for neglect. There are always reasons why people hold back, draw away, and do not cope. Though I had raged, fortunately it had all been inwardly, not outwardly directed at his sister, and felt as blame. The family grieved too, and as time went on I understood a little more of their story. I had really only seen Joshua; that was a narrow view. At the funeral I see a little more. I see his sister looking tired and worn. I meet family members from far away. I do not see her husband.

In the next months I see his sister from time to time. Every few weeks she asks me to buy them the discarded husks of grain from the mill when I go into town, that is all they can afford, but it is better than nothing to fill the children's bellies. I deliver it to the house, but never go in, and as she has no English we never have a conversation beyond a few smiles and handshakes.

One day I get back to our house late, after dark. And hear that Joshua's sister had been waiting for me for many hours. It is too late to visit her house, and because, in the morning, I have to take people to hospital, I plan to visit later the next day. She is already there waiting when I return from the hospital. She grabs my hand and struggling to communicate, despite her lack of English says with great determination,

"Come. Now".

She holds my hand tightly as we walk through the fields and bush paths in the scorching afternoon sun.

"My husband" She says.

She ushers me into the small dwelling that I last saw emptied of all but Joshua's blanket wrapped body. Her husband sits in the first of the two rooms. He is racked with coughing that shakes his thin body. I kneel beside him and feel his head. It is burning and beaded with sweat. I know that he must visit the nurse for antibiotics to fight the infection that is causing the raging fever. I urge them to go to see her. Meantime I share my dwindling supply of vitamins, and some of the decongestant that can give the ailing lungs a little relief.

There is little else I can do. I again urge them to see the nurse. I can see now why she avoided Joshua. He demonstrated the path it looks like her husband is taking. Any last vestige of anger melts away in me as I sit on the floor with them feeling the friendship that they offer me in sharing their suffering and their trust.

I return to visit Joshua's family once more before I leave. Now I truly see them, no longer am I tied to the narrow, limited view that anger solidifies. They express their hunger and their fear. I can do no more than just listen and be with them. Be with them in their little mud brick house, sitting on the sack that is the only furniture. I see the dark red-brown, smooth mud walls on which so little is hung, just a ragged chitengi and a dusty piece of basket work. On the floor lie empty clay food bowls, and battered saucepans. Then I see one other piece of furniture, a small table - the larder - on it are two small tomatoes and a little plastic bag of salt.

However, even in these bare surroundings is the warmth of welcome, friendship and the ever-present politeness, each of their children shaking hands with me, all saying, "Malka bwanji?" "Good morning, how are you?"

CHAPTER SIXTEEN

Stuck in the mud!

Driving back in the dark on unknown "bush" roads, my fears are eclipsed. There is no room, no time to be overwhelmed by fear here. As Amrita drives back from the hospital in the twilight, we notice a swooping and swirling of birds above us, as the swallows return. Their long journey from England is complete, and I have the consciousness that though now we are in the season of mud and hunger, with the English spring I will return with them and I am filled with a mix of bittersweet joy.

Though I am often with people who are suffering greatly, there is also much fun. Many people need to get to town and to the hospital and whenever we go, people squeeze into our poor beleaguered vehicle like sardines. The sickest go inside while the rest ride precariously in the back.

When I am not driver, I squeeze in the back too, enjoying the breeze in my face, the scenery and their mischievous humour. And when the rains come, I huddle with them under the few waterproofs anyone possesses, to try to keep out of the worst of the rain.

There is wonderful companionship, and I start to learn that in the company of friends almost every discomfort is bearable and even almost enjoyable if we join together in laughter.

We have quite a few close shaves with the vehicle, especially when the rains come as we struggle to stay on the rutted roads when we go off the tarmac out to the villages, collecting or returning disabled people.

Time is wearing on, and the struggles to renew my visa bring it home to me that I am now well past the midway point in my stay. I feel now that I straddle two worlds. I belong to both. This is bittersweet, I have come to love the people here, my friends here, as my own. And now I know my time is limited. In all too short a time I will have to leave, and there is much work to do. I now have to look for ways of teaching others the basics of massage for pain relief as well as the stretching and strengthening remedial exercises that are helping peoples overworked and pain-ridden bodies

More people are calling for me daily, and surprisingly, quite a few men are showing an interest too. We had expected that it would be mostly women interested in massage. People are also very interested in learning the exercises that can help their back troubles.

Much trouble is caused because they carry bulky and heavy loads on their heads. Also, at the start of the rainy season, everyone, man, woman and child, is working frantically in their fields. The digging, planting and the unaccustomed heavy labour takes its toll. Then there is the weeding!

Back problems are abundant and a few brave souls, hearing the word, start to look for me, including the men. Lying on the floor I demonstrate the exercises I learnt when I suffered with my back many years ago. Then I invite them to join me and try them out. They do! Amazing that in this patriarchal and rather chauvinistic society, they are willing to learn this from a woman.

Ndwali, when time allows, takes me to villages to meet members of an organisation - CBR (Community Based Rehabilitation of the Disabled). These are volunteers from villages throughout the area who are training in order to train others in various skills that they can then pass on to those in need. I am taken to villages to give and demonstrate massages and exercises. Members come with me to learn what is possible and how it is done.

I meet a gentle brother and sister. Peter has a wicked grin that lights up his face and cheers up anyone around him. He also has headlights that decorate his souped–up racing blue wheelchair (though thy are for decoration only). He, like many of the volunteers is himself disabled, only able to walk around on all fours. It is amazing how deftly he can manoeuvre himself around. With his quick wit and clever rejoinder he fills a room with infectious laughter.

His sister, Judith, is also keen to learn the ropes, and accompanies me whenever she can on my rounds in the sorely deprived area in which they live. Judith, a tall, slender young woman is an expert seamstress. Her clothes made out of the chitengi material in brilliant emerald green and aquamarine emphasise her sinuous body in unusual, elegant designs. She is lively and gentle and I look forward to working more with her.

One day I arrive in her area to find that I have queues of people waiting. Rapidly people clear a room in someone's house so that I can see a never-ending stream of people. There are also instructions to call on this person and that in other villages too. I have a roaring trade and Judith has plenty of chance to learn.

We all have plenty of laughter. Especially with the women, as behind closed doors I massage hips and teach the rolling exercises that will help relieve the pain. But the laughter really explodes when we finish with a rhythmic shake that turns into a dance, echoing all the dances women are taught to allure and keep their men. The women see me now as one of them, and I rejoice in their comradeship and laughter. I feel fully alive. When darkness and hunger eventually force us to stop, I find that, amazingly, I have done eighteen massages. I feel as if I could dance forever.

I have acquired a couple of regular "guides" out into the villages. Tom, who came with us at Christmas to Malawi, is amazing. He is small and wiry and full of energy. He is always ready to go anywhere at any time and to help as much as he can. Despite his lameness, he loves to dance, and while sober is an inspiration to all.

He is naughty too, I remember one day out in the villages when, while I was giving massages, he entertained the young with his dancing and the tape machine he had "borrowed" from Ndwali. When drunk he is to be avoided, though he is never nasty, just amorous! He desperately wants a wife. Luke is a young married man with small children. He is an ardent footballer and a keen volunteer to help people learn to cope with disabilities. He also wants to learn all he can to combat sports injuries by watching the work I am doing with my massage clients.

One memorable night they are both with me, guiding me to a village a long way from my usual area, on a muddy, rutted road. It is pitch dark. We are taking a terribly disabled man back to his village. New lush foliage grows high upon this little used track. It hides the ruts, and also I cannot see where the track ends and the ditch marking the edge of the field begins. The headlights shine dimly. I have to rely on Tom and Luke's shouted instructions as they peer out of the window. "Right, right, just a little". "Left now left..." "Right, no no, no, NO - LEFT....!!!!!"

Too late, they shouted right! They meant left! The vehicle slides away with me, down and down into the ditch. I struggle to hold the wheel. I pray it will not overturn. I cling on to the wheel as it tries to buck out of my hands and go into a fatal spin. I manage to hold it – just. We teeter on the edge of the track, the left-hand wheels just holding our precarious balance.

One by one all those who are able to, get into the left side of our vehicle, some crawl out the windows into the open back, the rest lean out the windows and squeeze their weight together above those left side wheels.

The vehicle rocks with every movement. But it holds, and their weight stops the vehicle from slipping further into the muddy morass.

I put the truck back into gear, pump the accelerator and slowly our poor old vehicle claws its way back to safety.

The adrenaline pumps through my veins, my passengers whoop with delight. This for them is entertainment at its best.

I might have made a rally driver after all!

However, we are actually glad of the mud, because of the food shortage. The crops are growing strongly and it now looks as if the spectre of hunger will not threaten them in the coming year. But for now we are deep in the midst of hunger because of the failure of the previous year's rains.

I had never experienced a food shortage before, and rarely experienced hunger. Every trip to town people ask to come with us in order to get maize for their families. It costs too much. More are asking us to try to get sacks of the rejected husks of maize from the mill. There is little calorific value, but because it contains a lot of B vitamins there is some nutritional value and briefly it fills their stomachs.

Day after day people come to our house to beg for food. Women show us their children's stick thin arms and legs; they open their own clothes to reveal sagging empty breasts and folds of skin over their bellies under which there lies no protective layer of fat and twist them around almost in a knot. Sores will not heal; coughs rip out from under sunken ribs. Infections run rife in their undernourished bodies.

"Njala" is on everyone's lips. "Hunger".

It twists me painfully to hear this day after day. I feel sick inside at seeing the suffering. I feel impotent at not being able to help. At times I want to scream and cry, rant and rave at anyone and anything. I have little money. I can do so little. Nothing to relieve this amount of hunger, and even then it is a painful decision whether to spend the little money I have entrusted to me from Amida on medicines or on diesel and repairs for the vehicle. All I can do is tend a few sores, teach a little massage, and listen to their stories. All I can really offer is friendship and say

"I'm sorry," with kindness as I shake my head.

Esther often goes to our cupboard and finds it bare. She knows the culprits who risk her ire; Ndwali or I have often given away whatever we could find. We all feel it deeply, and we also grow thin. Every day our one meal is stretched to feed the visitors that arrive at our house and sit around waiting.

I had not realised how the weight was falling off me until one day I see myself in the bath at the MPs house. Amrita, Esther and I look at ourselves, our clothes are hanging off each us, lack of food, long hours of work, and repeated attacks of sickness, are taking their toll. But in some ways it feels better to be sharing the hunger with our friends than remaining fat and comfortable. For me anyway.

In some ways I am glad to know what real hunger feels like, so that now when I hear stories of famine I don't turn away. I am glad I was there with my friends.

All of Zambia has been affected, and rumour after rumour filters through that famine relief is on its way. Nothing materialises. In the end Ndwali and Amrita start chasing up the office in town which deals with food relief distribution. Even during the midst of funeral arrangements and transporting people to and from bush villages, they make visits to try and track down the rice which is due in our area. They have found a special under-utilised scheme for planting sunflower seeds to make much needed cooking oil; but only hopes of rice, nothing has as yet materialised. The more they dig, the more they find that part of the problem is that there is no NGO - non-government organisation in our area. Only an organisation unlinked to government is allowed to supervise distribution of the food aid.

It starts to look as if Tithandizane might need to take on this onerous task. An irritated and frustrated MP, concerned for his people, adds his weight to the arguments trying to persuade Amrita and Ndwali to take it on. No one else is able and willing, and without an organisation to take charge, the people will stay hungry. Many people are already starving, surviving solely on mangoes. In the end it is the only way. Yet another dimension is added to the work of Tithandizane.

A famine relief committee is formed with members coming from different sections within the Tithandizane area. We are ready to receive the rice.

What a disappointment. We find out that the amount to be received is derisory; only five Kg of rice per family of at least ten people. The amount is based on old obsolete, inaccurate figures of population, but hopefully it will boost morale in the area. Decisions are made to offer some to the sick and elderly, while villages take turns to work for some of the food. This "Food for Work" scheme helps get some necessary jobs done, and means that the food is not just a handout, feeding apathy and taking away power from the people.

It is not an easy job; we have long journeys to check on the distribution of the long awaited rice, and future consignments of maize. We have to make sure that the scheme is operated fairly and that the requisite work has been done. There are plenty of teething problems in the distribution and supervision. Also people are so hungry now, that some might play foul to get hold of food for their families.

Sadly the amount received is always minimal, and there is little official support available for the starving in the form of social welfare. It is impossible to convey what it feels like to see people starving, to hear their pleas, to see their desperation.

As I write, my stomach twists with the memory.

This is no well-advertised famine, where pictures on television or in newspapers stir the Western consciences. This is a quiet hunger as people slid downwards in a spiral of deprivation.

Often people suffer in silence. Sometimes a neighbour will tell one of us about someone who particularly needs help.

One day Ndwali calls me to come with him, bringing my massage gear. He raids our near empty store, and we set off. On the way he tells me "Ambuya's" story. Someone came to him to tell of this old disabled woman who lives alone, has no food, and had not eaten for a week. Also thieves had stolen her whole crop of ripening maize. Ndwali has been to see her with some of the relief maize, and realises that some massage will help her greatly too. She has been crippled for a long time and can only crawl around.

We walk through her sadly dismembered crop of maize, jumping puddles as we go to visit her.

Her face shines with joy when we arrive, and she sees Ndwali again. She relaxes with a sigh of pleasure as I massage and ease some of her pain.

I remember sitting at her feet as she sits on her mud step, the sun shining on us. She relaxes and chats and laughs with Ndwali as I gently probe and stroke and ease her broken deformed knee. I look around; the ground is neatly swept, clean and tidy. Her neighbours care for her.

Before I leave, I give her the surprise of her life. I had been visiting this old lady for some weeks, and we had become friends. Friends enough for her to jokingly ask me to give her my chitengi as a leaving present when I say that this is my last goodbye.

I stand up and laugh, unwrap it from round my waist and present it to her with a bow. I smile as I write, remembering her astonishment and joy. To an old lady who has nothing and no one, and probably not long to live, this is riches indeed. So my chitengi in Amida colours with lotus blossoms did not return with me. I leave the lotus flowers in Zambia, in a place where they belong.

Amidst all the suffering I can remember much joy, laughter and companionship as people work together, and as I work with them. As I travel, I get to know the bush roads well. Even in these months of the rains I can avoid the worst places where the vehicle is likely to get bogged down or sucked into the ruts and ditches that, after storms, run as fast streams of brown water.

One day, I set out early to visit Anna in Mchala. I am enjoying the driving this morning, the sun is shining, it sparkles on the wet leaves, and, after the heavy rain of the night, the air is clear, before the heat settles in a misty haze over the foliage and the ground again returns to dust.

The drive is challenging; water runs fast in the deep ruts, there is little room to manoeuvre. I am full of adrenaline, my heart pumps fast as I hold the wheel tight and watch the road like a hawk for signs of crumbling earth that could pull me down into the morass.

Strength is needed as I near the school turn off where two wheels are two foot higher than the other pair. I guide them steadily, two on the bank and two on the ridge between deep ruts; I breathe a sigh of relief as I get safely past this obstacle.

The track is drying out in parts, but in others it is fully covered in water. I drive up slowly, deciding whether to go left or go right, this pool of water varies in its stickiness, and I have to pick the best side, then travel at the right speed, too fast and the wheels will spin, too slow and I will get stuck. Another trap avoided, I travel on.

The last bit is the worst. Soon it will be totally impassable. It is a long stretch of deep ruts, high banks and bends and curves, little time to think before each challenge. This is really like a rally. Today I am conscious that this may be the last time the vehicle comes to these villages until the rains cease and the ground dries out. If I make it this time that is.

At last I am onto the last bit of track, it smoothes out, I turn to the right over the rough grass to enter the village. I smile and relax. In the village I feel safe, the ground is packed firm, and in the morning sun the overnight floods have dried out, Anna's house is in view as I get ready to turn between the first two houses.

Then it happens. I feel the vehicle sink slowly and inexorably downwards. It stops going forwards, the front and left side just sink down; no amount of acceleration will haul her out. We are stuck!

We get out to look. Around us the ground still looks innocent, but there we are, the front left-hand wheel is up to its rim in mud, the right hand one is little better; more water seeps into the rut. It is full of soft slurpy, treacherous mud. A thick porridge that holds us stuck fast. Ndwali and I just look at each other.

"I'm sorry, I didn't expect this," I say.

Ndwali shakes his head "The water makes channels under the surface in the villages as time goes on, we should have stopped going off the track into the villages."

Tom jumps out and goes in search of sticks and stones that are carefully placed under the wheels to help offer purchase. I try the engine again; I put it in gear and rev, and rev and rev. No go. We just slide further in.

A few young men from the village venture over to see if they can help. They find longer planks to form a ramp for me to try reversing backwards and up. Up to their knees in mud the young men push and rock and struggle with this metal monster. I accelerate and rock myself, behind the steering wheel, willing our trusty vehicle to move.

No go, and the wheels slip sideways off the ramp down into the mud. More and more from the village come to join the fun.

We try again. No go. I sit and watch, the planks are again positioned, and to my amazement these strong young men bodily lift the vehicle sideways onto them. Once again I am called to the driving seat to turn the engine and to try to spur the reluctant monster to move. Still no go.

The hours pass. We try again and again, failing every time, getting deeper and deeper in. We all stop and wait a little, some go off, and some from time to time try moving around planks and stones. I am hungry, we left early without anything to eat and it is now late morning. I worry; there are people due in hospital. My hopes are low. I can't see a way out.

We wait. And then the oxen arrive, slipping and stumbling in the mud. My hope rises; they look sturdy and strong. They are yoked together and are further yoked to chains and to the vehicle. But they are reluctant to move, reluctant to pull this strange, heavy load. Their owner curses and encourages them; they dance around a bit, they move forwards, backwards, sideways, and finally haul with all their might.

Not this time.

But nothing daunted, the men get back to work and boards and stones are repositioned. Once again with their combined strength they physically lift the vehicle onto the boards and stones. They get in front of the vehicle, ready to push.

I am motioned to get in, and turn the engine. I am frightened, what if I slip forwards rather than rev out backwards and crush them?

The oxen are pulling from behind. They chomp and shuffle sideways. Will they pull?

My hope is all but gone.

I get inside and turn the key.

I rev the engine, find the gear, let up the clutch... The oxen pull, the men push, the engine revs - and revs... The reverse gear fights for purchase... At last finds it.

With a slow slurp the mud reluctantly releases her victim.

I reverse cautiously back the way I came. Then stop and rejoice! The young men are dancing, proud at showing off their strength. They are the victors! They persevered against the odds. They deserve a prize!

There is not much give, but my whole stock of condoms is given away that day!

CHAPTER SEVENTEEN

Mike's Story

...Such a beautiful picture through the doorway - the soft dawn light bathes the African landscape. In the middle ground a beautiful tree, and passing in front of it a slow moving oxcart. The night before too - before coldness pushed me into the house in the small hours, there was such a beauty and feeling of community in the scene. A huge long open fire in front of the house - the men seated on one side the women and children on the other listening to the choirs - one arriving on foot from a far distant village to serenade this wise and learned man...

Birthday! Thirty-three years old. Mike is in sparkling form. He is also delighted to have reclaimed his children from his ex-wife into the safety of his mother's arms, and the upswing in his health seems to continue.

It is a wonderful evening as I sit with him, his father and brother, and with the elders of the village, discussing the state of the world. This night I sit with the men. A log is brought for me to sit on; Mike and his father are on stools, while others sit on the mud step of Mike's house, forming a debater's circle. It is a mild evening after rain. The stars shine, but it is the dark of the moon. Mike's mother sits in the background, cuddling for his children, just listening.

Mike proves to be an excellent translator, fortunately, because he is the only English speaker in his village. It is one of the many conversations I have about "development". Most young people think that this is what their country needs most of all, and most of my conversations with them question this form this need takes, and how it is implemented. I highlight the plus points about living in their type of community while sharing some of the problems young people face in the western world.

These elders already hold a wider view and do question the type of development needed and what development could bring. Will it bring the much needed medical facilities and educational opportunities along with the income? They fear for their young people in this modern world. They worry about the drink and drugs that are a panacea for many nowadays. They worry about the eroding sense of community in the villages now, as well as in the towns. We compare the problems that face the young in our respective countries. They are shocked to hear about young people committing suicide, and the amount of mental illness that is prevalent in western society. It is a night of two cultures coming together and learning from each other and finding mutual cause and friendship.

Within days Mike takes a turn for the worse and is back in hospital.

It is the start of the season of deaths. The effects of the food shortage are starting to show; malnutrition is hitting many beleaguered bodies. The wet season brings out the mosquitoes in abundance as the lusher foliage and growing maize affords them ideal breeding grounds. Everything grows, for good or for ill. From the mud many other organisms find their ways into human bodies and it is impossible to avoid paddling in the mud. Every trip to the latrine in the midst of a storm or its aftermath involves a walk through a foot of muddy water.

In the damp air droplet infections spread numerous bronchial diseases. Sores from insect bites and constant wetness will not heal. Fungal and viral infections flourish. The numbers calling at our door with candida and herpes increase. The young and old and people with impaired immune systems are particularly at risk. These diseases respect no persons.

We receive word that Mike is sick, very sick. Amrita goes to see him in his village, and knows that he has to get to hospital. Maybe he did make the wrong decision; perhaps he should have gone for the biopsy. Perhaps it is the same as with Paula, TB of the lymph glands, perhaps there is time for him to respond to treatment. While Ndwali and I go to the funeral of the wife of a local farmer who is a staunch supporter of Tithandizane, Amrita, Esther and Gotami take Mike to hospital. She leaves him there in the care of his brother, promising to return the following day.

I return with her the next day, not daring to hope that he is still alive. Amrita had told us that he had been so sick she was not sure whether we will be visiting his hospital bed, or bringing back a corpse.

We make our way to the TB ward where he has been installed. Finding it means a walk through long, grim, grey corridors. All seems grey though outside the sun is shining. We go through a gate with the security guard and turn left to enter the ward. It is a long ward, painted a dull pale green. The overhead lighting gives a strange light. Battered iron beds fill the ward, and sometimes between them there are mattresses on the floor, squeezing in yet more patients. A mixture of smells assaults the nose, blending together in an indefinable mix.

The windows let in some light, and through them I can see yet another row of beds on the veranda outside, where the "fitter" patients are recuperating in fresher air. We walk the length of the ward our eyes searching every bed. Beside many beds sit a mother or father, sometimes on a chair, sometimes on the floor. Most of the occupants of these beds are young men, some seem little more than children. As usual the bundle of possessions wrapped in a chitengi lies beneath the bed.

The sight of these bundles always affects me, each one the symbol of a loving mother caring for her child. In them are pans and plates and mealie meal. They cook and try to tempt their loved ones to eat in the hope they will regain lost strength.

Mike is in a bed at the far end of the ward. This is the place to which they relegate those patients they have little hope will survive. He is alive – barely - but is not eating or drinking; he is nearly blind and devoid of speech.

His brother is distraught, no medical treatment has been given, and he is lying there in his soiled sheets.

First we must make him more comfortable; we know how humiliated he will be feeling. We beg clean sheets from the staff. I slip my arm underneath his arm, gently putting it round my neck; then slide it round his back and underneath his other armpit; then, putting my left arm behind his knees, I gently lift his wasted body in my arms, holding him to my heart. He, a grown man, feels as light as a small child. I hold him as Amrita and Brian change the soiled sheets, then lower him gently and carefully and prop him up so that we can give him some water, some life giving fluid, while Amrita feeds him a soft banana. He takes a little, reluctantly.

Amrita then goes to see the nursing staff to plead that he be given the TB drugs. Brian had clearly heard the night staff say it was not worth bothering, as he was HIV! Once the nursing staff see that people care about this man they agree to give him drugs.

We have other calls to make, so we have to leave him there, in the tender care of his brother. I leave sadly and reluctantly, wondering if I will see him again. More uncomfortably I leave wondering if we are doing the right thing, persuading him to live. Does he now really want to live? I am aware that at one point as I was feeding him water; he swore and turned away from me.

All we can do is wait and visit when we can.

A few days later we receive a desperate plea for help from his brother. Brian is exhausted and scared,

The hospital is a grim, dour place at the best of times, but perhaps a large TB ward is one of the worst places of all; the never ending coughing, the frequent deaths, the groans of pain. Traditionally a family member stays in the ward with a patient, sleeping at night on the bare floor under the bed. They provide food and change the soiled sheets etc. and sit in many hours of what could be called meditation.

Brian has spent several nights by Mike's side; he is now distraught, lost in fear and terror, and exhausted.

We visit.

Mike is now being drip-fed. He is unconscious, but from time to time tosses and turns as he lies there. In the corridor outside, Brian spills out all his fears. He is convinced that they, whoever they are, are trying to kill Mike. He is I think, misinterpreting the movements of staff and visitors, probably hallucinating too in his desperation and fear. He is just a young man, this is a huge task for him; he needs a break. Amrita takes him to friends of hers who have a farm, so that he can have a proper meal and a good night's sleep.

I take his place with Mike in the TB ward. It is an honour to do this for my friend. His friendship helped me settle in and get my bearings in what is for me a very alien environment. But more than that, I admire him for his determination that has helped the Tithandizane project to get off the ground. He is determined to ensure that others will not have to suffer as he has suffered. That vision and determination has helped fuel the creation of the project. His support for Amrita and Ndwali has been unwavering. He inspires us all.

While staying with Mike in hospital, I learn much more about how it is our way of being that is most important of all. I sit with him in his pain, hold his hand, meditate and quietly chant. I lift his frail body in my arms to change his soiled sheets. I talk with him, and cry with him. I had in the past listened to his fears, and heard his aspirations. So I am able to use this knowledge to reassure, and try to prepare him for whatever lies ahead.

Now he is silent, nothing more seems to need to be said. All I can do is be with him, helping him to face the death that is to come. From time to time I rest a little during the night, lying on the floor below his bed, allowing him to lie quietly when he finds peace for a little while. When I hear his tossing and turning in physical or mental discomfort I return to hold his hand and offer him my love.

I look at his face, his dark ebony skin contrasting with the grey of his sheet. His bones form an etching under its smooth canvas. He is beautiful as he lies there, and his closed eyes demonstrate a peace that was disturbed on my last visit. Then his eyes had rolled widely in fear, the whites standing out in the shadow of his face. Now his long lashes lie sleeping on his cheeks and I too feel a greater peace.

But maybe more important than the reassurance my presence gives Mike, is the effect of this care on others. The skeleton nursing staff is interested and intrigued. They are used to giving just the most cursory care. Understandable really in view of all the suffering they face. As dawn beckons we have some good, and heartening conversation about the care of patients and about Tithandizane. Their spirits are lifted too. Also, as they go out in the morning many families of patients speak to me, I can see that the down-heartedness has been breached a little, and several even said thank you.

Even weeks later I am reminded of that time by the family member of another patient who was there that night.

Above all, the thing that is imprinted on my memory is the sight of a dozen faces staring at me through the window that was behind Mike's bed. Just watching. It felt like I was a performer on TV. I had forgotten the window was there, and that on the other side of it, were the rows of outside beds. I was just being with, and caring for, a friend.

The shock of seeing the faces brought it fully home to me that this is what our work is about, and this is what my Buddhist training is for. It is not for doing any great deeds, or giving great teachings but for being able to do whatever is most needed at any given time.

Brian returns, refreshed after a good night's sleep, and full of good farm food. We all know it is just a matter of time before Mike's death, but Mike, in his fear of death and judgement day, is afraid to let go. Physically, too; he is being fed through the nose, belated care that just increases the vomiting and diarrhoea, and the time it takes to die.

Once again we question ourselves about whether it is right to persuade others to live. We question whether he would have been better dying at home in his damp dark house. There are always many questions, and no absolute answers. The reality of AIDS has sunk in at an even deeper level as I watch my friend suffer and draw near to death.

The reality hits home too as we visit his mother. I see the hope die from her eyes as she takes in the looks on our faces when we get out of the vehicle. This is worse for me than being with Mike in his dying. At this point, the only comfort I take is that his brother Brian, the young pastor, for whom this is the first encounter with the dying process at first hand, might be a more compassionate companion for others in the future.

A couple of days later I flag down a crazily driven minibus to visit Mike.

His life is still hanging by a thread. Again he is lying in his diarrhoea - no clean sheets are available - but our pleas bring some pads to place under him. As Brian and I gently roll him onto his side to extract the soiled sheet, the flow changes to blood. We know it will not be long until death claims him. Sadly, I cannot stay for long. Ironically this is partly because a wonderful troupe of actors from this hospital are due in our area the next day to put on a road show to teach young people, by dance and drama, about the dangers that can lead to HIV and AIDS.

Two days later Mike dies. The very same night that takes Joshua beyond his suffering and into the peace of death.

As soon as the word of Mike's death comes, I go to join his family in their vigil. Again there are long hours waiting, sitting in a room bare of all but sackcloth - and, a rare thing here, some lino, in what had been in life, Mike's own bedroom. This is the room where, not long after I arrived in Zambia, I spent many worrying hours. Here is the room where our friendship was sealed. This is a close friend I am grieving.

This funeral is for me a very personal affair. The grief is heightened by the fact that he had regained consciousness just after I left the last time, and in his last two days was crying for Amrita and myself. If only... But I know that it was impossible... Other needs intervened.

I stay for a few hours, then leave to collect my sleeping bag as I intend spending the night there. I think it will be a comfort for his family that I join them in their vigils. It is a confirmation of friendship and a demonstration of respect. I feel it is expected of me. And I want to be there for them and for me.

Mike's funeral brings to life some of Ndwali's explanations of the funeral process in a discussion we had a few days previously. Perhaps Ndwali had been preparing me as he described how the proceedings are orchestrated to allow the grieving process to take place and how the community supports the bereaved through the process.

There is a beauty and feeling of community in the scene when I return to Mike's house. In front of the house there is a huge long open fire - the men are seated on one side the women and children on the other. Mike's coffin has now arrived and lies inside the house, in his old bedroom. His mother and close family sit around the coffin, keeping him company on his last night in his house.

I do not wish to intrude so, for now, I join the village women sitting on the ground in front of the fire. They smile and make space for me. We sit listening to a choir from the village. Then another choir arrives from a far-off village, their beautiful voices touch me deeply. I am amazed how far they have travelled to honour Mike.

Darkness cloaks us in its velvet blanket; the stars shine bright, the waxing moon peeps at us as we sit. The air grows colder and we draw in closer to the fire. I seek out my sleeping bag, watched in amazement by the women beside me. Perhaps they have never seen one before. Their pleasure brings me new warmth as we wrap ourselves together in it and continue our vigil.

We stay wrapped together until, in the early hours, they return to their homes offering me a place to sleep the night. I refuse. It is cold and briefly I am tempted. But instinctively I know that my place is to lie with his family and keep Mike company. It is a precious in-between time as one life finishes and life for others begins without the beloved being there. It is a time for tears – from time to time these erupt suddenly from the mourners, and then voices join together wailing in harmonies that rise and fall, eerie and haunting.

In the cold small hours I go with the remainder of the women into the house. We squeeze into the outer room. We are packed like sardines; our bodies stretching out together round the walls, the centre of the room a jumble of legs and feet.

In the inner room Mike's mother and close family wait beside his coffin. Throughout the night there is a kind of 'master of ceremonies', who keeps the mourners in order, directs proceedings and removes a drunk who had tried to join in with one of the choirs. The choirs take turns through the night; singing hymns with lovely harmonies that sometimes lull us into a brief sleep. Their skilled harmonies contrast with the more homely singing of us mourners in the house. We are never allowed to sleep for long, beside the hymns, there are rousing sermons. There seem to be about six different preachers haranguing us through the night!

The wailing starts at dawn. It wakes me from a short sleep. At first a lone voice, a mother crying for her lost son, then as the dawn light creeps in the open door others join in. Full of sadness my tears slide down my face as I too confront a dawn in which there is no Mike.

Then I look through the doorway and see a beautiful picture. The gentle dawn light shines on the African landscape, painting it in colours of subtle ochre. The dry and barren bush lies in the background while in the middle ground a beautiful tree stands proud. Passing in front of this is a slow moving oxcart. I can imagine the Buddha sharing such scenes as this, and I feel close to him as I confront the reality of death.

I go to the latrine, and returning, feel the urge to sit a little while with Mike's coffin. I enter his room; his mother sits there with a few companions. She looks up as I enter and smiles a little in welcome.

"Kalopantze" "Sit down". She says.

My place is indicated and others make space for me. It seems as if every person in the room has a set place and now I am not allowed to move from mine. Long hours on the hard floor follow. The others see me wriggling in discomfort, and to my surprise, despite being in front of the coffin, show me how to lie to relieve the pressure on the bones. Kind hands physically re-arrange my limbs as I struggle to understand their directions. People in Zambia often lie rather than sit, not only at funerals, but everywhere. I had found it strange; but now I fully understand why.

I regard Mike's coffin. It is very smart; its polished wood shines and has big brass handles. His family could never have afforded this - it is provided by his employers. Another sword goes through me. Mike had an important job and was the main breadwinner in his family. He was the Headman's son, and therefore his passing has to be conducted in style. I think of Mike, he had style.

His mother laughs gently at me. Even in front of Mike's coffin she takes pleasure in making fun of me as she points out to newcomers that I don't eat meat, and even more strangely, don't take sugar in my tea! She makes a face. Zambians love sugar. We smile. We are connected, sisters, mothers together. I think Mike will be smiling too in his coffin. He loved to see his mother tease me.

She pulls me out of the room briefly, to share a bowl of porridge, and then we wait again. The morning passes, we wait as mourners arrive, each one erupting into wails of grief that we echo and harmonise with. Each person is shown her place; Mike's mother is showing an authority that I had not seen before.

Word comes. All are assembled. It is time. We leave the dark room and for a moment the sunlight blinds us as we duck through the doorway and join the waiting crowds. Mike's mother and senior women are ushered into our vehicle. The choirs perch precariously in the back around his coffin. Amrita drives slowly into the bush. I walk close behind amongst his family and friends. Again it is a woodland burial site. It feels such a long walk to his final resting-place. I see another grave made ready to receive yet another victim of this thing called AIDS.

Mike's mother calls me to her side in the shade of the tree, to sit with her as we listen to the many speeches. There is one from Amrita; she has been requested by the family to make one, and I had heard her practise it in her limited Nyanja. I am saddened. I know it is not the speech she had hoped to make. Mike had wanted her to speak out about the truth of his death from AIDS. Later I learn that the family was divided as to whether the word AIDS could actually be spoken. This adds to Amrita's sadness, her own failing health had denied her the chance of being with her friend's family in their vigils. Repeated bouts of malaria and other afflictions had weakened Amrita's constitution.

Finally the wreaths and flowers are given to the mourners to be laid on the burial mound - Amrita and I laying one together; paying tribute to this friend whose courage and dedication inspired both of us. He leaves a huge bequest to his community - the Tithandizane project and the hope it brings for a happier and healthier future for his people.

CHAPTER EIGHTEEN

The Nkoma Family

Sometimes the sight of so much illness makes me so sad, even in the midst of laughter. ... Their pain seems to link with my own loneliness that occasionally hits me. A very inner loneliness in not being able to share how I am feeling in the way I have been used to. People here deal with things much more pragmatically and stoically. Yet, in a way I feel I am getting stronger as I have to call on my own inner resources, and, in truth, are they my own? And I am very much not alone!

As the old year draws to a close, a new friendship grows. I met Mrs Nkoma and her smallest children the night I arrived at Tithandizane. I see her every day drawing water, and her children, if not in view can be frequently heard, as they call and play. It is these children's arms that surround me many times as I sit on the step of our house, their small hands pulling and tugging and plaiting my hair. They chat and question me incessantly, laughing when they see I cannot understand. They are the cheekiest and most beautiful children I have ever seen. They became my friends almost the day I arrived. The friendship with their parents grows as the New Year dawns and dark clouds gather.

I first meet Mr Nkoma a few days after my arrival. We take him to the hospital because the nurse cannot find a way to stop him fitting. He is not conscious, so he does not really meet me. We fear for his life. The nurse has no idea what is causing the fits. As we drive to the hospital he lays in his wife's arms in the back of the vehicle. The nurse sits on the other side of him, we are all praying that we will get to the hospital in time. I can feel his shaking in the seat behind me.

I am scared. This is my first visit to the hospital and this is a strange road where we often have to swerve sharply to avoid nameless things, or are roughly thrown about as we hit potholes. I guess I absorb the atmosphere of fear in the vehicle. Mrs Nkoma is on the edge of panic; the nurse sounds almost angry as she speaks loudly and vociferously.

Amrita concentrates fiercely on driving. She is tired and that is why I am accompanying them, she wants me to drive them home. Maybe this is also why I feel scared. I fear my first night drive on this unknown road. I feel safer as we enter town with its few streetlights. We bump our way up the rough road to the hospital; the sight of its brightly-lit entrance cheers me. Surely he will find help here.

The nurse goes in and then re-appears with an orderly and a trolley. They help Mr Nkoma onto it and wheel him away. I wait in the vehicle with Amrita, resting a little in that midnight hour. Sometime later the nurse re-emerges. He is settled in and we can leave him for now. Time will tell whether he will live or die.

He survives, and a few days later returns home, but I do not see him again for a couple of months. Just before Christmas he comes with us to the hospital to have some X-rays done, and to get his prescription checked for his TB. I am surprised when Mrs Nkoma asks me to take care of him, she has some urgent shopping to do and so she asks me to help Mr Nkoma around. He walks with the aid of a stick, his legs are swollen and walking is difficult for him, which is why we have not met each other since that first night.

I had not really seen him that first night. It was dark, and he was soon whisked away into the hospital. He looks younger than I expected, he appears quite well built, and is taller than average. He also is dressed very smartly, I guess that is because, in his fitter days, he worked in town; most of the men I know in at

Tithandizane are part of the farming community. He is different from most of the men I have met in other ways too. There is a gentle air about him.

And he speaks so nicely to the nursing staff and the others we travel with. He exhibits a certain shyness, which seems to come not from a lack of confidence, or from fear, but from a concern for others. I can tell from the way he speaks that he is an educated man. Not from his spoken English, that is very unpractised and he struggles to find the right words, but by the type of questions he asks as we wait. I can feel his genuine concern that I am well and happy in Zambia. Also I know from the questions that he sincerely wants to know more about the world I come from and the wider world beyond that.

In him I sense an acceptance of his illness, which does not come from apathy. He is prepared to do whatever is needed and accept whatever comes. We speak of the pain and swelling in his legs, and of my discovery that massage can help a little. We make arrangements for me to visit whenever I can to see if it might be useful for him. We enjoy each others company, from him I learn more about Zambia, and his work, while he is keen to learn more about Britain and especially Scotland where I used to live.

I visit his home a couple of days later. His wife is outside on the step, cooking on the charcoal brazier; her children are playing nearby and grab hold of my hands in delight as I come up to the step. Mrs Nkoma rises, removing the pot from the coals. She wipes her hands on her chitengi before holding one out to me in welcome and continues to hold it as we stand there. She smiles with pleasure and I wonder why I have not visited before. Possibly that was wise, not intruding too fast, coming when asked and not before. Now as I arrive I feel I am truly welcome, not just as a "helper" but as a friend.

The house is similar to ours. There is a front veranda, and a door leading to a central living room, while to either side are small bedrooms. Unlike ours it is full of furniture, a sturdily made settee and armchairs with big dark red cushions, and a small stocky table in front of them. There are posters on the walls, and a small oil lamp on the table. She ushers me through the curtained doorway into her bedroom.

Mr Nkoma is stretched out on the bed with his legs raised to try to ease the swelling. He smiles,

"Welcome",

Then swings himself round with some difficulty to sit on the edge of the big bed.

Mrs Nkoma brings me a chair that just squeezes into the room. She seats herself on the small bed that lies against the other wall.

"I am sorry, I am not so well today, and I have to lie down for a while." He apologises.

"Is it the legs?" I ask.

"They get worse, and some sores have broken out".

"Look" Mrs Nkoma points to his ankles,

"What are these? The hospital does not say, the nurse does not know."

I look at the grossly swollen legs. They look as if they will burst with all the fluid they retain; and they are covered by wart like growths, that have become weeping sores around the ankles.

"I don't know, I am no medical person, I just do a little massage, and help with driving and first aid and whatever I can."

They are not dismayed; in a way it does not seem to matter to them what I do or don't do. It seems that what they want to do is talk. They talk together with me, telling about some of their hospital visits and about the progression of the illness. Then Mrs Nkoma leaves me, encouraging me to try the massage while she tends to the food.

I sit on the single bed facing him and try to raise his foot. It will not lift more than a few inches and his leg is very heavy, so I slide down and squeeze onto the floor between the beds, then gently manoeuvre his heel into my lap. Then avoiding the sores, with very gentle massage, softly try to persuade the fluid to move in an upward direction.

"It's not good." Mr Nkoma says from above my head.

"I don't know what these things are, but they are not good."

I look up and meet his eyes. He looks at me calmly; I give a wry smile. There is nothing I can say.

"I get sicker all the time. It is hard for Mrs Nkoma. She worries. She tries to find a cure."

He is just telling me and in his words I find no self-pity, just a compassionate concern for his wife.

This is the first of many such conversations. As I massage he talks. He has a fair command of English that improves each day. His wife speaks little English, but she too, starts to learn some. It grows into a routine, I arrive and go into their room and we all talk together for a while. Then she leaves while I offered the massage, and he and I talk.

His curiosity about our life in the West is insatiable. We have many fascinating conversations and much laughter, gentle laughter. He is an unusual man. His love for his wife and children is one of the deepest I have seen. As time goes on he starts to share his fears and talks through decisions he has to make. All he worries about are his wife and children, how they will fare when he is gone. He knows he will die. He had not expected the disease to progress so quickly, but he has accepted it. It is only a question of time. The question is how to prolong it just a little.

Mrs Nkoma's tears affect him very much. She loves him deeply, and cannot hide her fears. She spins around and around worrying and trying this and that to try to help him. There are practical worries too, less than a month previously his young brother died. Already his family is under pressure, and they had relied on Mr Nkoma's wage coming in to help them bring up his brother's children. Also Mrs Nkoma has no father alive to help take care of her. Although at present they are fortunate that he has a job, and sick pay to provide for them, the house comes with the job, and raging inflation will soon erode the value of any pension. The longer he can live the better, and besides it gives his wife some of that precious, yet also misleading commodity – hope.

Their current dilemma is whether to try village medicine next, one of the local healers, the Ng'angas, or to try yet another hospital. They decide to try the hospital.

Mr Nkoma comes home the same day. He was not even admitted. They said there was no hope, nothing to be done. No cure for the lymphatic leukaemia that leads to pain in his body and causes it to fill up with fluid. The only hope now is village medicine.

I continue the massage routine, it gives some physical comfort, but the real comfort I think for them, is in the routine of having a space to talk and most importantly to find some laughter and lightness between the three of us. Then, when Mrs Nkoma leaves us, he can unload and share his fears with me. Her turn comes when she walks me slowly home. She holds my hand as we walk, and lets go some of the tension that spins her round in circles.

"Come again tomorrow," She says each time I leave her.

If I do not come, she will come for me. She stands there waiting outside the door, sometimes silent, sometimes chatting and laughing with Esther. If I am out she leaves a message reminding me to come. However this is a two-way friendship. Our laughter is shared. With them I do not feel so alone.

We explore the world together in that little room. We philosophise and put the world to rights. We drink in each other's lives. I learn about their love and their young married life. They learn about my children and this Buddhist life I pursue, though it is a bit beyond their comprehension, so steeped are they in Christianity and all its "mores". I learn more about the belief systems that people use to make sense of the troubles that face them. Alongside Christianity, Mrs Nkoma still has a belief in the old religion, hence her recourse to native healers, and fear of witchcraft and curses. She fears, like so many others who have loved ones who are sick, that illnesses are a result of curses. It is a way of making sense of the number of diseases that afflict some people.

Sadly the deterioration in Mr Nkoma's health carries on apace. He has to return to the hospital and needs transport in our vehicle. I drive it round to stand beside his house. He waits in his wheelchair on the veranda and we lift him out of the wheelchair to sit beside the passenger door. I have difficulty working out how to transfer him to the vehicle. We cannot lift him under the armpits, as a huge painful swelling in his shoulder is painful to the slightest touch. At first I stand back and watch Mrs Nkoma and his friends puzzle how to achieve the move from wheelchair to the high front seat. One man tries, but fails to lift Mr Nkoma's heavy, water sodden body up into the seat. Mr Nkoma screams out in pain.

Shouting, "No, no."

"Wait, don't try any more." "Get Ndwali" I scream out in turn.

It is the first time I have seen Mr Nkoma display such pain, and fear. His face is twisted in agony, his body shakes and beads of sweat stand out on his forehead. I stand there, my hand on his shoulder trying to offer calm and making sure no-one else tries to move him. Ndwali arrives and I explain my plan. He gets into the vehicle and from the middle of the front seat stretches down to pull him up using the waistband of his trousers. Meanwhile I brace myself under Mr Nkoma from below his buttocks and lift upwards. I am so glad that my physical strength has increased and that in the past I had had some training how to lift. This time we make it.

All too soon he is no longer even able to get from bed to wheelchair on his own and several times a day the call comes for Ndwali or myself to help with the lifting. He will not trust anyone else. The strange agony in his shoulder gets worse. Inexplicable pain which the hospital tries to help alleviate by first a plaster cast, and then binding, to no avail. No matter how gently I try to lift, his face betrays his agony, and yet no matter how clumsy I am he never goes beyond gentle admonitions.

In conversations too I am awestruck by his gentle acceptance of his wife's demands that he try this hospital and that, in the search for the cure he knows can never be found. I never hear one complaint, despite all the agonies he has to endure. I learn about love.

At one point he and Mike lie in beds, side by side in the same hospital. I go by minibus to the hospital, to see Mike before he dies and to bring TB drugs for Mr Nkoma. Even in hospital we have our usual routine. The three of us talk together about the hospital, the treatment and the ward. Then his wife goes to the shops for food, leaving us to talk. He speaks of his fears for the children, and for his wife, and I leave with his words in my ear.

"Look out for the children".

Mrs Nkoma joins me in the walk back to the road. She speaks of her fears for him, and what the test results will show. She sends me off with instructions for her mother on how to care for her growing maize – what fertiliser to give, and when. Her concern is feeding her family.

All around us the cry grows even louder.

"Njala". "Hunger".

A dark February dawns. Things get much worse.

Mr Nkoma returns from hospital with all hope lost, weaker and in more pain than ever. Three times a day either Ndwali or myself are called to help lift him to change his soiled bedding.

Finally one evening a few days later, his pain has increased so much that his wife is agonising whether he should stay in their house and suffer, or risk a long journey to another hospital where at least he can be near family and will hopefully receive palliative care. I am against making the journey; it is a hellish drive at the best of times. This is the season of the rains, and the hospital lies at the end of a long dirt road. A road with a corrugated surface consisting of a maze of ruts that even the best driver can never hope to avoid. It judders and jars every bone in one's body. How will it feel to a man for whom the slightest touch is agony?

Yet that is her decision. She is adamant, and he is no longer capable of making any decision in his torment. We struggle to get him out of the house, his eyes wild with fear. We take him out on his double mattress, trying to cause him as little pain as possible and give his body some protection from the bumps. This time he travels in the open back of the truck.

Late that dark night we set off. Under my breath I utter curses. Even on the tarmac road we cannot dodge every pothole. The dirt road towards the hospital is even worse; more holes have appeared as the rainy season progressed.

Mr Nkoma screams in agony at every bump. His mother and his wife lie on either side of him in the open back of the vehicle, trying to protect and comfort him. As I drive, Ndwali and I bite our lips, and dare not look at each other. I cannot afford, anyway, to take my eyes off the road in front as I slowly negotiate the potholes and ruts. I cannot avoid them all.

I boil with rage. I scream inside at his pain. I hope that in this life, I might never have to make such a journey again.

Yet also I know that it is impossible for adequate care to be given at home. This is the best hospital around and there will be some hope of a dignified death. Finally the long three-hour journey is at an end. We ring the bell at the emergency door at the back of the hospital. An attendant comes and quickly finds a trolley, and wonderfully hears our request that we carry him in on the mattress to avoid having to touch his agonised body. Gently between us all, once inside, we roll him onto a bed in a clean, quiet ward. I leave him with his eyes still rolling in agony.

I leave my friend not knowing what the last hours or days of his life will hold.

We start the long journey back.

Some days later I learn that he had been given the painkillers needed to take the edge off his raging pain. For a special two days he regained his consciousness and lucidity. And died with his family around him.

I go to his funeral. I make the long journey to his home village in the hills. I travel in a vehicle from his workplace, full of his old friends. It is a large funeral, and another grave under the trees. Before he is carried to his plot of earth, I sit along the wall, with many others, his body before me. He lies in the main room of his parent's house. The coffin has not been delivered yet, so he is still wrapped in the blanket I know so well. - The one that covered his bed back home. His body is still large with fluid and curled up from the pain. I feel as if he is here with me.

This time, because we still wait for the coffin food comes before the burial. We are all taken to various houses in the village to eat our nchima, and then return to sit outside and wait while the body is prepared for burial and placed in the coffin.

It is outside that my tears start to fall. We line up and walk slowly round him as he lies in his coffin. His eyes are still swollen lidded, but his face is now at peace. As I walk slowly past, my emotions are mixed. There is relief at seeing him in peace at last, his eyes no longer haunting me; however I also feel apprehension for his family at what the future might hold for them.

I did not properly see Mrs Nkoma. She was in a side room with his family. At the funeral, she was not allowed to speak. I saw her body, but not her face, as in an old tradition she was led around, her shaven head covered by a chitengi for the duration of the funeral. That way she can look at no other man and no other man look at her. But even under the chitengi I can see her slender form convulse in tears.

I do not expect to see Mrs Nkoma for some weeks, as she had explained previously that, after his death she would be beholden to his family, and her life would be governed by their whims. They will probably not allow her back into her home, so her mother remains there, caring for her children and tending her crops, until the time for harvest.

She does in fact return earlier than we have expected. It is good to see her back! It is a relief to hear more about Mr Nkoma's final days and know his pain had been eased and that he had been able to truly be together with his loving wife and family. In the end he had a gentle death. I am relieved too, for her smallest daughter. She, usually so bright and bubbly has been quiet and still. No longer racing around playing. She misses her "Atata" "Daddy".

Also she misses her sister who had been sent away earlier to live with another family member who is childless to ensure that she will get some good schooling. In Mrs Nkoma herself there is also a change. She is no longer running round in circles with fear. Facing his death has brought her peace, and determination, to do all she can for her family. And right now that means raising her crops.

She has her mother beside her. Her mother does not speak a single word of English, yet her kind, warm smile always raises similar warmth in me. Through all the painful visits during the last week of Mr Nkoma's life we had felt a comradeship. Our shared glances and bows probably expressed more than words can ever do. Mrs Nkoma also has something else to sustain her. A gentle belief in God, and now she gives herself to that, as she accepts all as "Gods will", while doing the best for her family. Though she also knows that in reality it is the will of her husband's family that will ultimately determine her future.

Mrs Nkoma is coping bravely, trying to provide the best future possible for her children, knowing that they will probably have to go different ways, in different homes within the family. This is a usual custom in this society. Here one's brother's children are thought of as one's own. And no matter the distance of relationship one is also still family. Likewise if one is adopted, then the whole family adopts you. One does not even have to be a blood relative, as I had discovered with the Ndaka family. In friendship the Nkoma family have also adopted me.

I continue to visit regularly. We sit and chat as she holds one of her children tightly between her legs and plaits her hair into one of the beautiful intricate designs that decorate many women's and children's heads. A few weeks after her return, when I go to return a cardigan I had borrowed from her, she brings out all the family photos. Pictures I have never seen before; pictures of them both shining with health. In one is a chubby Mrs Nkoma that I can barely recognise. The picture had been taken not very long before I met her. There is also a picture of them with his pride and joy, his motorcycle, and photos galore of the children. She introduces me to others of her family, and to his, including his young brother who died recently.

At the same time she is preparing herself for another loss. She is choosing photos of the family for me to bring back to England with me.

CHAPTER NINETEEN

Celebration

The day dawned unmarred by the rain clouds. The rains are a little more sporadic now. We squeeze as many as possible into our vehicle and set off. All along the road, from many miles away, people are walking, keen to be part of the big event. This is a huge event, thousands upon thousands of people are milling around; Vehicles crowding into a muddy field. Many reunions going on in an exuberant atmosphere.

How does one have dinner with a chief? When I enter the house I am shocked to find that from somewhere Esther has acquired a small table, and it is set for two; the chief and myself.

I have never met a chief before, but I have heard plenty about how one must treat a chief. In this area he is king. He is owner and carer of all the land and protector of the people. He is a dispenser of justice, who can actually over-ride some state decisions. He almost holds the power of life or death. He is to be addressed as "Nkhose" which means Your Royal Highness, or to salute Him, "Yo Jeri".

However, leading up to that meal, there is "THE MEETING".

Many people are expected for the meeting, to be held in the Tithandizane project room. Headmen and members of the Tithandizane committee come from many different villages. As usual mostly men, but more and more women are being encouraged to take their part in all types of committees. There is a thriving campaign to bring more equality to decision-making processes. More vocal and adventurous women are needed to take part. While we do have some wonderfully active women in Tithandizane, they are all too few.

When Senior Chief Nzamane 1V arrives for the meeting his uniformed aide leaps smartly out of the vehicle to open the door and let him descend. He is a distinguished figure and the flash of white hair above his forehead adds to the imposing picture he presents. He is simply and smartly dressed and his upright bearing makes him stand out from the crowd. And his size! He is very tall, broad, and of muscular build. He radiates power.

All people bow and call out, "Yo Jeri" then stand back to let him enter and take his seat in the room.

He offers greetings to his headmen, and to the officials from "Microprojects" - the organisation we are all hoping will assist our project. The meeting seems to go well, many important decisions are made about the needs of the community and what is possible to be achieved. Chief Nzamane then gives a rousing speech encouraging and exhorting the community to pull together. He also voices his frustration. Several times both he and officials from the Microprojects organisation had been hopeful that such a project would come to fruition, but the villages had failed to come together.

Divisiveness in the community had led to the failure to provide both the consensus of opinion and the materials that are needed to make such a project happen. He warmly praises Amrita and Ndwali for helping bring the people together to get this far.

But first, much more hard work is needed to fulfil the requirements of "Microprojects". The people have a lot more work to do; much more sand and crushed stone is needed for the buildings and possibly more bricks. Also there has to be a guarantee of land. Here a local farmer speaks up; he will gladly exchange his land, which is ideal for the project for some his neighbour, the MP, is using - if the MP is agreeable. The Chief thanks him and assures him that some suitable solution will be found.

The Chief then says that he will grant this land to Tithandizane in perpetuity. A grand promise indeed. This meeting, despite the demands it still leaves on all echelons of society, feels like a real breakthrough.

We walk outside still talking, and Amrita invites the chief to eat at our house and to our delight he accepts. We know Esther will have food ready, but I am not prepared to be eating together with the chief! It is a delightful meal. He is a gracious man, and friendly. As we converse I am impressed by Chief Nzamane's knowledge of his country and his subjects, and his concern for them; both in this region, and in the rest of his tribal area. He is also interested in the rest of the world and keen to hear more. He is larger than life. He appears a stern and good man.

It is wonderful that a couple of weeks before Mike dies he can see his dreams for Tithandizane getting closer. The surveyors come to map out the land. The Chief's Aide, his Kapaso, comes with them and they have their instructions – to give a good sized portion of land to Tithandizane.

The gifted land starts some fifty metres away from the clinic buildings and lies adjacent to the road. This gives easy access particularly necessary for the sick to get to hospital when needed. To the rear, the land stretches back towards the hills - five hectares in total. This is an extremely generous grant from the chief. Security is ensured for Tithandizane for the years to come.

It is all processed correctly, so that there can be no arguments in the future. The surveyors come with measuring tape and all their instruments, while the young men hammer in stakes to mark out the limits. It is a glorious day. We have great fun accompanying the surveyors as they mark out the land. We share our dreams and make future plans in the knowledge that one major step towards them has been accomplished.

I next see Senior Chief Nzamane 1V in full regalia, at the N'kwala festival. The people here have many ways of expressing their joy and one of the biggest expressions of this joy is participating in N'kwala. This is the biggest event of the peoples' year and is almost upon us. N'kwala is on every one's lips.

Everyone asks, "Are you going?" and "Is Amrita dancing?"

Their gestures say it all, as they rock their bodies in an impression of the dance. They love to see Amrita dance. In her dancing she has reached the hearts of the people. Groups from two different villages have pursued her to join them, and between bouts of malaria she has spent much of her spare time preparing.

She is famous for her dancing, and not just among the villagers. Senior Chief Nzamane IV himself enjoys her dancing. He is the host of N'kwala, held each year in its special ground, at the centre of his tribal area. All the chiefs of the Ngoni, including the Paramount Chief, Chief Mphazeni himself will attend. Chief Mphazeni is the Chief of Chiefs; Senior Chief Nzamane is his second in command and sits beside Chief Mphazeni's throne. Other dignitaries from both the local area and from further afield will also attend, including the president of Zambia's wife, Vera Chiluba.

Despite her failing health, Amrita has been practising for weeks, whenever she gets the chance. Her determination is enormous. We take the dance troupe to the festival ground a couple of days before the event so that they can polish their demonstration of their skill. All the other Ngoma groups are there practicing their skills too.

Everyone goes equipped with cup, bowl and spoon. This is an unusual thing. Normally everyone eats communally, sharing plates. But this year the cholera is reputed to be close at hand. The fear of cholera is almost palpable. Day by day people speak of it in hushed tones, reporting rumours of its advent. It can kill within 24 hours if the diarrhoea and vomiting is not counteracted by re-hydration. It is not so much a village disease; it is mostly a disease of crowded insanitary towns and because of it the street vendors are disappearing off the streets of Chipata. We no longer dare treat ourselves to the home baked maize meal fritters and cakes the small children hawk by the roadside.

Despite these fears there is already a festive atmosphere at the site. It is the first time I have seen people walking around in traditional costume. Little groups are practising their steps, circling around, swaying and stamping. A few women are also dressed in animal-skin skirts, and with breasts bare, dance along with the men.

Some tents are erected, though most dancers are accommodated within the village. In the field of dance itself a huge pavilion has been erected to house the chiefs and special guests. The ground is drying out a little now and the blue skies look set to remain. Excitement is in the air, and anticipation. Adrenaline is flowing as they practise, all hoping to get an opportunity to display their skills. Not all will have the chance as there are far more troupes than time allows. Each troupe longs to dance in front of their chief and demonstrate their skill and their loyalty.

On the big day itself, I have a very strange sense of déjà vu. We leave early; the vehicle is crammed full of villagers, excited like children at going to the spectacle. Slowly we crawl up the muddy track towards the field of action, amidst the hordes of brilliantly clothed subjects of the chiefs. We squeeze into a narrow parking space in a crowded parking area. We are not used to seeing so many vehicles. Many have travelled long distances for this annual reunion, and come from all over Zambia and beyond. Ndwali and I creep around the edge of the arena and try to get a closer look at the dignitaries,, wary of being chased away by the attendants.

The joyful atmosphere reminds me of the Scottish Highland games I attended each year with my husband, when he was an exiled Scot in London. The circular arena is just the same; the awnings under which sit all the chiefs and the dignitaries have the same look of precariously, erected shelter and comfort. The chiefs are magnificent.

Whereas in Scotland the men had walked around in flying, swirling kilts. Here the men wear skirts of animal skins, heads and tails sashaying as they walk. There are furs of many colours and dimensions, some with ancient histories from generations of Zulus. Ornate headdresses dignify many of the heads.

Staves and drumsticks are twirled; the dancers turn and twist around to the beat of the drums, just as in Scotland the kilts swing to the skirl of the pipes. Whereas in Scotland athletes compete in running and tossing stones and caber, here the troupes perform amazing acrobatics in an arena that takes on a life of its own.

People sit in large groups all around the arena, comparing the abilities of the troupes, and catching up on family news. On the outskirts many small businesses ply their trade. It is an exhilarating day. Ndwali introduces me to this person and that, and to many members of his extended family. His father is there too, and at an opportune time takes me across to be introduced to the president's wife.

And Amrita dances. Though her face shows the strain of illness, she dances, and as she dances, her synthetic furs swirl with the rest.

The next day Ndwali and I return to collect Amrita's belongings. She became sick after we took her home at the end of the day - malaria again. Many stayed on overnight in and around the arena, including the Chiefs. Many troupes were still dancing the next day, including a wonderful woman's group. It gives me a little more time to stop, enjoy and study the movements and resonate with the rhythm. I am also grateful that it gave me time to meet again with Chief Nzamane, and to be his driver, as first we return firstly, his belongings to his palace, and then the man himself.

This would not be the last time I would be his driver and receive the chance to hear a little more, of what this dignified, caring man has to say. He is a big man and not just in size. I had and still have great respect for his wisdom.

CHAPTER TWENTY

Joy

... Even in the midst of suffering there is another side to life: the laughter Ndwali brings to the patients and nurses in this over-crowded ward is healing in itself. And as we walk by the windows in the corridor outside, an exquisite dawn sky catches our eyes — threads of rose pink and pale blue with the silhouettes of trees and hills building a breathtaking picture. A painting being created before our eyes. We share our delight in it. Just as in the midst of all the car frustrations yesterday...Ndwali drew my attention to the swirl of multicoloured butterflies in the bushes beside us. As they examined the car he turned and caught the wonder in my eyes at the beauty of the landscape, and the banana trees that still fascinate me, their fruits always look to me as if they are growing upside down! There is so much beauty here if only we can see it...

One day, at the height of the mango season I am out in the bush. A man, waving frantically, jumps out nearly in front of our vehicle from an almost invisible side path.

He jumps into the vehicle, beside me;

"Come, come" he pleads.

I gather there is an emergency. Cautiously I follow his instructions and navigate a tiny overgrown path till in near darkness we reach a small village. The entire village seems to be surrounding a young lad lying on the ground. He is biting his lip and groaning, I can see that his right leg is held straight by a neatly made improvised splint of branches tied by creepers, and covered by a wad of leaves. They remove this pad and I can see a splintered bone protruding through the torn and bloody flesh.

Gently they lift him into the back and I proceed slowly to take him to see the nurse. As I expected he needs to go to hospital. A few days later when we are back at the hospital we call in to see him, and find him smiling happily, his leg held up in traction, sharing laughter with a ward full of children who have also fallen out of mango trees. Apparently this is a seasonal occurrence!

One wonderful old lady also lives on in my memory. I go to visit her in her village when I receive word that she is badly crippled by arthritis

"Can massage help her?" I am asked.

"Perhaps"

I respond cautiously; by now I am aware that it is not wise to raise hopes too far as I never know what I will find.

She is on the floor of her one-roomed hut. It is an old-fashioned hut; small and round like a little beehive. It is nearly totally bare of furnishings and she lies on a mat surrounded by several concerned women.

I feel around her leg and knee very gingerly, she winces at the slightest touch, and the odd angle in which she lies indicates that her grossly swollen knee is certainly not due to arthritis. To me it looks as if it may be broken. I can do nothing to help, and try to persuade her family to take her to hospital, to no avail.

It takes much persistence by Ndwali later in the day to persuade the family to let us take her to hospital. She then has a long stay in the women's ward.

We visit her a few times, and find that unlike the silence and sadness of the men's ward there seems to be much companionship and conversation and often laughter here, even though there are not enough beds. She lies on a mattress on the floor in a far corner of the ward along with many others.

Ndwali and I are in the hospital as dawn rises one day, and we creep into the ward to visit her. She is already awake and as I hunker down to sit with her on the floor; she chuckles with pleasure. Even at that early hour, Ndwali soon has all the patients, and the staff laughing. I am deeply touched, when just as we are about to leave, Mrs Munagra catches hold of my arm and leads a prayer of thanks to God both for gifting us this wonderful world, for her treatment, and our presence at Tithandizane.

Why we are in the hospital at dawn is another story:

The knock comes at the end of a long day; we are well ready for bed, I am even in my pyjamas. There is an insistent banging at the door.

We open the door.

"My wife has gone into labour, she was told she must have this one in hospital or she might die, please help?"

I had met this pleading Dad and his wife some weeks before, when they had moved to the area. They had been advised that she must go into hospital when her time comes as her life could be at risk. We had promised to help. He is very frightened; she was well into a labour that had come on prematurely. He had left her some hours previously because it was a long walk from their village to Tithandizane.

Once again we have a night trip, way into the bush to collect the Mum and take her to the hospital. Once she is safely ensconced in the maternity ward, Ndwali and I make our weary way home in the early hours.

A couple of hours later another knock on our door! Another desperate man, his daughter is in labour, and has been, for a dangerously long time.

Sleepily Ndwali and I gather our things. Amrita is still sick, and Ndwali and I have a lot to do in Chipata anyway, so it has to be us! We are tired; we had not anticipated such an early start, or a drive out to a village to pick up a pregnant mum.

But the effort is well worth it, as she too is soon safely ensconced in the maternity ward. We get our jobs done in town, and late afternoon return to the hospital to see how our patients and our Mums are doing. We are met with beaming smiles. Yes, it was worth it; the scales with death have been balanced a little. They and their little daughters are all well, and the first one delivered is ready to make the journey home.

My journal reflects my elation:

"Then it was home with a delightful new baby and a shining new mum. A lovely drive back too, the most wonderful skies in each direction, blue in front, jet black dark clouds, some with a silver lining, indicating the lowering sun behind, and to the south, all the hues of pink, from pale grey-pink to a glorious rose; soft and billowing in contrast to the stark black of the northern clouds. Later that night too there was a sharp clear sky, where the stars shone out. The length of the Milky Way was stretching out to infinity, and various nebulas could be seen so clear to the eye. It was too, a night of music and laughter as we all sprawled across the floor. Sweet relief..."

I feel as if I have a grandchild. Affection has grown between these young parents and myself.

When we collect them from the hospital they spread their joy around to all they meet. We get to our house and I find I have people waiting to speak with me and since their needs are now paramount I miss the new parents leaving. When I hear I am concerned that a newly delivered woman is walking such a long distance within hours of the birth. But to the women here this is normal; pregnancy is not regarded as a sickness, and generally giving birth seems to come more easily to these active women.

It is not long however, before I see the father again. He has not come because of problems; he is there especially to see me. He has a special request. Will I name his daughter? Will I visit to give her a name, preferably my name, in the hope that it will bring her health and happiness. I feel hugely honoured, but I am left in a quandary. Should I call her Modgala or Louise?

When we visit the family to give the name, there is no choice really. Already she is being called Modgala, so Modgala Louise it is! She is so tiny and cute. I can see her now, as I write, and feel her tiny form swaddled in my arms. I just pray she will survive. Her parents and sisters beam with joy as the sun shines. We sit and talk and exchange presents. I give a chitengi painted with brilliantly coloured birds, while I receive some of their precious first crop of peanuts. They pose for photographs to record this day of joy.

Some days later the parents of the other baby born that night also come with the same request, so now there is also a Louise Modgala in Zambia.

Two precious presents are left behind me in Zambia, who, if we had not had the vehicle, would probably not be alive, and very likely their mothers would not have survived either.

In the weeks before I leave many more joyful days ensue. Tithandizane has the land, and now it has to be planted! First there are the banana trees; a full vehicle load of them, a gift from Amrita's farmer friends in Katete. We have a day of fun as local youngsters plant them around the far perimeter, capering and displaying their strength as they dig and haul the large trees around. Food for the future!

Another day Amrita and I go to villages where she has found the healing bush "saboodang". The children carefully dig the young roots that are the most suitable for transplanting until the back of our vehicle is full. They will be used to form a perimeter hedge round most of the land.

That day comes; it is a slow backbreaking job, transplanting them, until the local school turns out to help. For two days the whole school plants them, all in exchange for a football! This is the sign of the times; the schools have so little indeed. It is a couple of days of great fun and learning as the work goes on. Amrita has full scope to put her teaching skills to work as she teaches about the value of these bushes for those who are sick, and the need to take care of one's health.

The local school welcomes her back - to run an art competition. Each class is making posters demonstrating health themes. It is very touching to see how the children are so grateful for the art materials. Simple crayons and paints and papers. There are none available in the school, or in their homes. It gives Amrita the chance to do more talking and more teaching, hopefully sowing the seeds that will help protect some of this growing generation. They produce some wonderful posters too.

This is not the only opportunity Amrita has of putting her skills to use with the children. Amrita has a great belief in the value of "Woodcraft groups"; she had run one before, in England. They are a pacifist alternative to Scouts and Guides. I must admit, that although I had never seen one, I had my doubts whether the people here would be interested. I am glad to say I was wrong.

Even on the first day a dozen children arrive, and soon there is a waiting list. They bring us joy, as they display their joy, in the games they play and as they proudly clutch the fast growing mustard seeds they have sown. They also receive art materials and treasured green shirts from a group in England that links the children from two cultures in friendship. As time passes, in keeping with the ethos, more parents get involved too, and so the teaching goes on.

Amidst the joy, we are all suffering and Amrita is very sick. In fact we are all getting sick, with either respiratory infections or malaria. Ndwali too has a frightening bout of malaria. The malaria is getting more virulent. In particular it damages livers, where the parasite likes to lodge, and hide from the chloroquine given to kill it off. Then, one day, some weeks later it returns and we have another bout of malaria. Alternatively, in our small, overcrowded house a mosquito would bite one of us, pick the parasite back up, and deliver it on to the next person. Round and round in circles it goes.

We visit many villages, where the children's swollen bellies and yellow tinged eyes and skins testify to its enduring, damaging presence.

However, we have one tool in our armoury: Milk thistle; but we only have very little.

One day Ndwali receives a wonderful gift. A very precious small package from someone he had met when he was monk at Amaravati monastery in England. This is a packet of milk thistle seeds. Lovingly he plants and cares for them.

This is not the only gift that Ndwali receives from Amaravati monastery. They sent him back with tapes of dharma talks from the monks. We also receive through the post inspiring teachings from our own teacher - Dharmavidya. Whenever I get sick or sad Ndwali seems to be able to produce just the right tape to help me carry on. I have treasured memories of some evenings listening to those tapes.

But I must admit we do not only listen to serious tapes. On the visit to Mfui Ndwali and I had discovered our shared love of music. In England, in the sixties, when I was a teenager the forerunner of reggae music - Ska, triggered my appreciation of music. The wonderful beat stirred my blood, and led to an enduring passion for reggae music, particularly the inspiring music of Bob Marley. In Zambia this is reawakened, and I am now introduced to Rhumba.

Some nights, the music goes on and we dance away our blues, and release the tensions from the day, dispelling the despair and frustration, which can otherwise threaten to overwhelm us.

Tom often joins us; despite his lameness he sure can dance, moving to the rhythm, and leaping around in a way that defies any attempt to label him as disabled. Though if he arrives after having had a few drinks, he has a few tumbles too.

Other nights we come back to the house, collapse on the floor, and in the soft light of the kerosene lamp do our planning and reviewing.

However, frequently this disintegrates into laughter and sometimes we literally roll around as we let off steam. This is notably aided one time by a letter I receive from one of Amida's resident poets. He was also on the first "Activist Week" in Amida France with Amrita and myself.

Stanley is a wonderful performance poet. I have been blessed to see him in action a few times, and can imagine his mobile face and gestures as he performs his pieces of art. His words can paint pictures, sometimes in very angry words and couched in a black humour that suits our life in Tithandizane very well. He is due to perform at the upcoming Amida conference back in England, and here we have a sneak preview. His influence lingers on for nights to come.

Amrita shows that she is no mean poet either and entertains us with rhymes that make us dissolve into fits of healing giggles.

As time wears on, every passing day is precious. Every meeting has to be treated as if it might be the last. I realise the truth of impermanence in every step I take. This is a very precious time. My journal records:

"So many sights now are being etched on my brain. Perhaps this will be the last time, or for a long time till I come back… So many beautiful sights. Yesterday, seeing the children at Kulanai dressed up for the Nyau dancing under the tree, and in the soft light behind me the hills and the grass roofed huts, painted a pretty picture. Then this evening when walking, the African savannah landscape captivates me. Stark hills against the rolling Savannah, sparse trees stunningly shaped. It reminds me of the Grand Canyon at dusk. No camera and no film could catch its beauty. No money could ever buy this sight. No medicine could ever provide the balm to the soul that truly sees and experiences the deep joy this sight brings."

CHAPTER TWENTY-ONE

Student Days

...It is all so moving, the sincerity of the prayers, before meals, and at night, us four women praying together for peace and a relief of suffering. It is testing too, for me, all the questions about my Buddhist beliefs. And it feels somehow good to map them onto my Christian ones. The two come very close together here for me. The essence, the kindness and the love are one. As I talk, teach and massage, this essence is with me, and there are no real barriers, no barriers of race, religion or creed, just our love and our humanity, and our aspiration to help others have a fuller life.

My work encompasses all dimensions of society. One day I receive a request to visit the mother of the MP. She is a wonderful, formidable old lady. Crippled with arthritis and very forthright in her likes and dislikes. She does not like modern technology, motorcars and modern medicine. But she is willing to give my massage and me a go. She loves it. Every visit ends with tea and much laughter. She keeps up a running conversation, pouring out her heart even though we both know I cannot understand a word. It is a kind of counselling.

In fact this is what I find more and more. As I massage, some people talk, spilling out their joys and fears, finding a witness to their suffering, while others, silently, let go of their pain.

One man from whom I learn more about the hardships in this country is Mr Nkanimose. Mr Nkanimose is a tall, distinguished looking man in his thirties or forties, with a broad smile; who has a very good command of English.

His story is a bitter one. He had been on national service as a young man, when one leg was bitten off at the knee by a crocodile, while his other was badly mauled. He lives in constant pain, and often walks long distances from his far off village, on his crumbling artificial leg. As a younger man he had hidden his anger in alcohol, as many do here, growing ever angrier as the value of the pittance of his pension diminished.

Despite his disability he struggles, along with his elderly parents, to grow enough to feed his extended family. Many people have extended families, often one or both parents have died of AIDS, leaving the spouse and children to be cared for and fed. It is a terrible struggle for the women especially, and part of the projects forward plan is to help them develop income-generating ideas. Mr Nkanimose is very involved as a committee member of both Tithandizane and CBR (Community Based Rehabilitation of the Disabled).

The plans we discus in our more serious times often focus around the work of CBR. This is a very vital link with another organisation, which Amrita and Ndwali had forged in the early days of Tithandizane. I had met the Finnish representative in Chipata early in my stay when we talked about our work and our presence in the villages.

A memory that lingers of that conversation was her appreciation of my fortune in actually living with the people in the bush villages and therefore getting to know the people as I worked with them. I felt her regret, that based in town, like the majority of people in Aid agencies, she rarely has a chance to experience the work at grass roots level, and build the friendships with people that make the work fulfilling.

A physiotherapy-training day is being planned for CBR in our area! Two members of CBR from town are coming to give training to the volunteers. About fifty people are expected and food will need to be provided.

Fortunately Susan is back. She looks well, rather thin, but full of energy. Susan volunteers to organise the cooking, as the training is being held in the school quite near to her house.

On the day we have dozens of people to collect, particularly those who are themselves disabled. Amrita and I take turns driving. We deliver a few groups to the school, and then:

"Oh no! Something's wrong, I'm losing power"

The poor old vehicle goes slower, and slower, and close to our house, half way to where the event is being held, grinds to a halt. Reluctantly everyone clambers out and, by the roadside they try to find a little shade from the burning sun.

I look for shade too. I feel hot and sick, another battle with the malaria parasite being fought in my body. I sit beside the back wheel waiting to try to turn the engine when needed but longing to return to my bed. I know this is just not possible, people still need to get to the training and it is quite likely I will be needed to help during the day.

Ndwali and Tom open up the bonnet and start poking around, delving in the dark. We all have much to learn about engines and this is a new conundrum. Time passes, still no response from the obdurate engine. We scratch our heads. Then a wonder turns up in the shape of Isaiah, the MPs driver. He knows more than we do, we hope. Steadily the numbers sitting with us reduce as people disperse to their homes; a good thing, really, as already the numbers have already exceeded eighty. Fortunately Amrita had stayed at the school on the last trip and they are able to proceed without Ndwali and myself as once again we play the waiting game.

There is little specific training that can teach us how to cope with all the different situations we are faced with. But I am certainly glad of the Buddhist training I received with the Amida Order. In particular, learning to be accepting of whatever occurs, treating it all as practice. I had also fortunately started to learn to have just a little more patience. Though, those who know me will probably testify that I still have much to learn about this!

Isaiah fiddles around with this and that and the hours pass, I turn the engine again and again, until finally, at last, the engine roars into life and we are on the road.

When we arrive, there is a classroom full of disabled people patiently waiting too. While the physiotherapy teacher talks of technicalities and demonstrates theory to the volunteers, I have been volunteered to teach basic massage and exercises to the disabled. It will help their communities if they find out more about the benefits of massage and exercises and in turn teach their families how to help. It is my first time demonstrating these to a group this size, but there is no time to get nervous.

"Malka Bwanji" I greet them as I enter the cool blue classroom.

"Nalka bwino" They reply, just like dutiful schoolchildren from the rows of desks they are sitting at.

Time for action: "Can I have some help?"

We push back the tables back to make a large space in the middle of the floor.

I remove my chitengi with a flourish, shake it out and lay it on the floor.

"Who's first? "

Nervous giggles and blank looks greet me. But I know what I am doing - I look for some of my clients amongst the throng and catch Jerome's eye.

He smiles and gets up eagerly. "Yes, please".

I have a willing guinea pig.

"Would you mind explaining in Nyanja what I am doing?" I ask him – I know he speaks good English so I cross my fingers.

I'm fortunate, he proves a very able translator, and has a great time explaining what I am doing to the onlookers. I am not sure exactly what he says but there are lots of "Ahs" and bursts of laughter, so I think they get the gist of things. Jerome is good to work with as a client, keen to learn and able to direct my hands as I massage and gives me useful feedback. The group laugh to see us lie down on the floor side by side, but watch intently as we demonstrate the exercises.

I had met Jerome some weeks previously when I visited some villages that were new to me. He came into the hut I was working in to ask if I could help at all. Many years ago he broke his back and has been in extreme pain ever since. Simple massage loosens up his taut muscles, and then he is able to do a few basic stretching exercises that loosen them further easing the painful pressure. He finds that afterwards he is able to move about more easily and with less pain.

His enthusiasm, explanations and translations of my instructions, prompts others to come forwards and try a little of the same.

Next I get a couple of chairs and demonstrate how it is possible to massage even over clothes and in a sitting position. Anna in Mchala is with us and she allows me to demonstrate the pain relief massage that helps her bound joints.

I then encourage others to have a go. We practise feet and hand massage on each other, learning to get the feel of massage and the muscles and bones that lie beneath our skins. In fact the time runs away far too quickly as more and more people come forward with their questions and sharing their difficulties. People are enjoying themselves, both in the giving and taking; not all can be worked with on the day, so we make a list for me to visit.

Time to go home. The first people get away OK. But then once again we are waiting. And waiting. We fear the worst. A passing car stops with a message; yes, the vehicle has broken down again! Amrita eventually appears in the MP's rather smaller vehicle. Once again the MP' driver has come to the rescue. The vehicle soon gets crammed full of people needing to get home, including Anna, who has probably never been out of Mchala in her life and now, to her delight, will have a night at our house!

For some of us there is no room. We will have to walk home. But we are not too sad, even though we have a long walk ahead of us. We are feeling high after the success of the day, and in no hurry to return to our homes. Ndwali, Gotami, Tom and myself refresh ourselves at Susan's house and then in the dark walk back, singing and laughing as we go. Despite all the breakdowns it is a very happy day, and a successful event.

CBR has a very extensive training programme. In the first weeks of March, arrangements are being made for the first residential course in our area. This will be about Cerebral Palsy and Learning Difficulties.

Ndwali and Amrita have been negotiating with one of the schools to utilise some of their facilities. The school is also situated in an area where there are many adults and children suffering from physical disabilities. This is due to the more limited vaccination programme available when there was an influx of refugees from the wars in Mozambique some years previously.

There is much work involved in arranging this event. Messages need to be sent out notifying the volunteers to ensure a representative from each part of the area attends. Stationery is needed for the students, as well as provisions for twenty people for five days. Finally it is all ready and waiting.

I am given a great gift. Amrita and Ndwali are too busy with other work to be able to attend full time, so I go as the Tithandizane representative. I am to be a student together with Zambians, on a course, that is in the main to be conducted in their own language, Nyanja.

A real case of reversed roles; here, others have the task of checking up on me! They have to check that I have understood what I am being taught, and whether I have understood the conversations and the assessments that ensue. I think they enjoy the task! I certainly do, and though my ability to speak Nyanja is very limited, I am getting to understand more and more.

The first day is the only one in which we are wholly based in the school. It is rather fun sitting at the school desks and looking at the blackboard! I feel like a child again and am tempted to dissolve into giggles. George stands beside it asking questions and writing on it relevant responses, outside the sun shines, inside in the coolness there is the squeak of chalk on board and hesitant mumbling as we try to get a grip of the subject with explanations in a mix of English and Nyanja. George is a townie and for him, English is his first language so he too finds Nyanja difficult. Ndwali has to play translator most of this day.

It is the only full day of lectures and seminars in the classroom, where we learn about the basic stages of child development, and the warning signs to look out for that suggest some aspects might be delayed. It is not dinned into us by rote, our own knowledge, our shared knowledge is drawn out via probing questions from George and Elizabeth his fellow tutor.

We talk a lot and laugh a lot; we start to think about why disabilities have occurred, and how they can be prevented, and how we, as volunteers, can help with that prevention, and help others to do the same.

We explore how we can encourage pregnant mothers to go to antenatal clinics, have their inoculations, eat wisely, avoid certain herbs and medicines, and go to hospital where possible for delivery; particularly if the mother is small or has complications in the pregnancy. We think about how we can encourage mothers to go regularly to child clinics so as to keep a check on their child's health and get the appropriate immunisations.

The next part of the day focuses on how to identify signs of cerebral palsy and learning difficulties;

also how to separate out any displaying signs of mental illness, or "strange behaviour" as they call it. I find it very touching to hear mental illness called strange behaviour. Having worked for some years in Britain with people labelled as mentally ill, I was used to a lot of terrible prejudice, ignorance and fear that often set people suffering from mental health problems apart from the rest of the community.

Here there is a much greater acceptance and gentleness towards the relatively few who are afflicted in this way. In the main people with mental health problems stay at home and are contained within the community.

In the hospital in town there is only one small in-patient ward for those suffering from mental illnesses.

One of the main objectives of this training is to identify children with learning difficulties or cerebral palsy early. Volunteers are trained to observe them in their villages, schools and clinics. Then an assessment can be made and a plan put into action to enable them to counteract some of their limitations and live a full and independent life from as early an age as possible.

The emphasis is firstly on teaching ADL - Activities for Daily Living. These activities start from the basic abilities to wash and dress, progress to being able to work in the fields and for some, learning workshop skills, so that those capable are able to earn a living.

The afternoon of this first day prepares us to see some people who are coming to the school the next day for assessment. On the remaining days we will be going out into the villages to interview families and make assessments there. First we have to learn how to take the family history, then how to make an accurate assessment of the child or adult's difficulties and design a course of action to assist them in learning activities that will lead to more independence.

Before we go out into the field, I am invited to give a little input, bringing in my counselling skills experience to give suggestions about how to approach the families, build their confidence, and draw out the information needed.

This is wonderful for me. It taps into old learning and helps me understand more, as well as bringing into perspective, many of the things I have been witnessing over the last months. We have a test; I am relieved that I do not do too badly, or too well! It is a great leveller, learning together. Perhaps, with hindsight, one of the most useful things about my presence in the group is that I am no better than them. My fellow students can see that we are not miracle working strangers with all the answers. To help people's suffering we need to share our experience and learn together and from each other. We learn together, live together and play together for these five days.

The next day, we sit on rush mats outside in the sun as people bring their children and the trainers demonstrate how to make and record an assessment, and then we take turns in making observations and suggestions. The sun shines as we listen and observe and learn. The following days bring a mixture of sunshine and heavy rain. We wait and talk and then when the ground has dried a little, and the clouds have dispersed, we walk out into the villages.

Long walks. A crocodile of students and tutors doing the rounds! They live on in my memory. Blazing sun beating down, beehive shaped grass-roofed houses at the side of us, groups of students sitting on the bare earth, sometimes silent, sometimes darting questions or responding to them as they observe and examine a client, or question a family. Then the long walk back, going over what we had seen in little groups of two or three, or just laughing and enjoying the scenery, the sun and the comradeship.

Living together, we share our whole lives in those five days. We eat all our meals together, the porridge, with bleary eyes in the morning, mid-day nchima at our desks in the classroom and our supper at little tables at night. For most of us there is more food than we are used to in our normal lives. There is lovely ritual in the way we hold the bowls and pour water over each other's hands as we wash them before and after the meals. We say grace together and pay honour to the food we receive. We queue up in the mornings to use the bathrooms, where we are kindly given bowls of warm water by the local people who cook and take care of us.

We four women sleep together in a row on the floor of the school office. We say our prayers together as we settle down each night, all of us commiserating with each other as the mosquitoes attack us voraciously, and in the morning we rise with a groan from the concrete hardness of the floor. Friendship grows there. It does not matter that three of us are students, and one is our teacher, or that they are black and I am white. We are four women together.

Elizabeth is a special needs teacher. A robust and elegant young woman with long delicately plaited hair and a wide smile; she cares deeply about the children she teaches. She lives in town, and is also very much involved in teaching with CBR. She is delighted that at last Ndwali and Amrita have managed to get some deaf children from the area accepted into a residential special school, where they will have a chance of a more fruitful life.

Patience is our neighbour, and is the new nurse who has recently arrived at the clinic. The number of patients calling day by day had warranted a second nurse, so she got the job. She is gentle and quiet, a contrast to Margaret's loud and argumentative persona. Not long before Patience moved to our area her husband had died, and now she is struggling to bring up her four children on her own, while not being in very good health herself.

Joyce I met some time before when I visited the women's group she had started. She has a strong determination to improve the lot of women in Zambian society. In her village she is a driving force. She is a strong and determined character. She has needed to be. Of the five children she has borne, only two survive. She knows much about suffering.

However she knows that something can be done to alleviate some of that suffering, and that learning both about skills and health care can help prevent the suffering of others in the future. She and her group are going to be the first recipients of a sewing machine and materials with which to produce useful items bearing health slogans.

In Zambian society, men and women lead very separate lives, and to an extent that is true here on the training course. We are accommodated in separate areas and in our "office" we spend time together as women, sharing our stories, plaiting each other's hair and in my case giving massages. But in addition to the seminars, assessments and meals, we join together in the entertainment, formal and informal. Life in Zambia is nothing without some musical entertainment, and that goes for training courses too.

On our first day one of the villagers arrived with his homemade three-string guitar. His beaming face as he strums and plucks and draws out a multitude of tunes stands out in my memory. We sit listening to him and chatting under the trees many a time as we wait for the next meal or activity to begin.

That is our informal activity. On other nights Amrita has arranged for the Munagra Drama group to come and entertain us. We can hear the drumming and chanting over the roar of the vehicle's engine from quite some distance away. Then we listen and sway and chant as they perform. The drums and the dances of these vibrant young men have stolen my heart, they even help me forget the weakness and pains in my body as the malaria parasite attacks yet again.

It is a wonderful feeling, to be a student again, and to be accepted. They prove that by the gentle teasing that goes on. They reckon that I definitely exhibit strange behaviour! I don't take milk and sugar in my tea!

I will always remember Peter's grin as he says that.

Like a baby I can't do some of the most basic things either! Like eating sugar cane properly. Definitely I am mentally retarded! I soon learn how to do that one. I become adept at stripping off the outside of the cane to get at the sweet and juicy pulp inside. My mouth waters at the memory. They even got a photo of that, when one day they manage to pinch my camera. The pictures show the many wonderful laughing faces of my friends and fellow students in Zambia.

I write in my journal at the end of the course:

".... (It is) good to learn alongside others. good to feel so accepted, just as me, not as this white newcomer, The joking shows it and it feels so good......This kind of programme is the hope for the future, a better future in this, and I guess, other countries, real advances and empowerment.. Not for me, here, overt Buddhist practise, and yet it is here in my actions and deportment, in honesty and answering questions, without pushing my beliefs in this deeply Christian country. It is a gentle line to tread, to be true to my Buddhist faith, and to be honest without alienating others, and in accepting them as they are, being accepted as I am. There is beauty in their practise too, as well as the heartfelt prayers, so many burst into song. Hymns known and unknown to me resound, and often link to music and dance, a dance that contrasts with the erotic Zambian dances. So much music and dance here, maybe this is because they face death so often. There is a fragile hold on life here, death is ever present."

The student days heralded the beginning of the end of my stay in Zambia. The goodbyes began there. It was the fruit, of what had been for me, a flowering in Zambia.

CHAPTER TWENTY-TWO

So many Goodbyes

Early morning, and it feels like France or Jesmond Dene, the sound of the birds in the trees, the feel of a cool breeze on the skin. I am at Ndwali's family house again...It gives me a very strange, bittersweet feeling, these echoes of France and Jesmond. Part nostalgic, part longing and part a sadness that this will be the last time I stay here, Time draws on inexorably. I will leave behind another family here where I am no longer just a "guest". The murmur of voices, still mostly unintelligible, is no longer strange to the ear. I can pick up more words though I am far from speaking them. But I know now that with another stretch of time I could learn much more. Bittersweet too are the repeated questions. When do I go? When will I come back? It's hard not being able to give a fully concrete answer, just hope very much to return. Also too the knowledge that there is so much to do, yet also I know how much there is to do elsewhere.

Tears are close to the surface in my last week. With each person I speak to I realise how soon I will be leaving. On the one hand, I long for home, to see my children, my friends and my Sangha family, and I know I need to return: my strength is failing as I keep getting sick. On the other hand I am loathe to leave my friends. I feel the pressure and strain Amrita and Ndwali are under. I want so much to help lessen their load. I feel weak in my selfishness and longing for home. Yet I also know I have work to do back home and need to talk about their plight in Zambia and maintain support for them from afar. I will miss my friends and the joy and companionship I have shared with them.

The goodbyes take many different forms. Few are formal. A couple of days are spent shifting sand and stones with laughing young boys, and an often pensive Tom, who knows that time is running out in his attempts to convince me I should be his wife. The people do not want to let me go. Quite a few regret that they have not found me a husband to make me stay. Members of Tithandizane doubly regret not accepting the very generous offer of twelve cows for my hand in marriage!

It is very poignant walking far out in the bush for a last time, visiting my massage clients, and hoping that more people will come forward and learn massage skills and put them to good use. As I walk I can see the sky changing, as the weather systems reverse. People are looking forward to the end of the rains, the end of the mud and mosquitoes; several villages are still unreachable by vehicle, life is still hard, but I can see the new maize ripening.

I have at last tasted the sweetness of cobs of maize toasted on charcoal, black on the outside and juicy inside. I ignore the fact that my stomach is not too pleased with this assault and ejects the unaccustomed food with alacrity! The new season of groundnuts has begun. I will never forget my surprise at the taste of fresh groundnuts; it is so different from that of the peanuts we are used to in the West. I even get a taste for boiled groundnuts in the final days. Sweet boiled pumpkins are now on everyone's plates, the pumpkins' dark exterior skin hiding deep orange, floury textured flesh.

The spectre of hunger is fading away, as is the cry of "Njala".

On another visit I come away with some things in Amida colours. The hats! All thirty-eight of them, lovingly stitched by a now radiant Paula. She still has problems with the TB, and might not live for long either, but for now she has a new lease of life. Her child is back with her, and she has some borrowed time to make peace with her world. Beautiful Paula, we shared many of our womanly secrets, befriended each other, and one evening when all seemed dark, we had looked at the moon and found Quan Shi Yin to be there beside us.

Tears are close as I say goodbye to Mrs Munagra and her broken knee. She gives me a heartfelt hug, something practically unheard of in their society; it says more than any words can ever say.

In the same village I visit other friends, friends with whom at one point I had been bitterly angry. I had come to know Joshua's sister much better, and come to understand what lay behind her neglect. From seeing beyond my anger a sense of humility has grown in me. We can never know the whole story, and no matter what anyone does, or does not do, we are only human, we share a common frailty, and at any time we can only do the most we are capable of. I had learnt much, and had much to thank her for.

I go for a last meal with Susan and her family. She is determined to do something for me. We have met a good few times since her return, and she has shared much about her ongoing struggles. Since his son's death, her husband has turned more and more to drink. Jealousy and bitterness are eating away at him. However, I can also remember, despite his drunken railings, the large slow tears that rolled down his face as we went to collect the body of his child. He, in his way, is still grieving. Susan has done hers and returned to the world. I have every confidence that whatever she chooses to do she will no longer be in danger of the terrible grip of apathy and oblivion.

The last visits to the MP and his family are moving; especially to see Ambuya the final time. As soon as she sees me she calls for soap and hot water, and makes herself comfortable for her massage. She talks and laughs, and teases and shares; but this time she cries.

"Why do I have to go?"

The sad look on her face haunts me, I feel bad about leaving my friends, knowing their needs. But even then I know I have to return to heal and to tell their stories.

Ambuya calls me back just as I am about to leave and presents me with a brightly coloured cloth; a precious purple and black chitengi, which now graces our cushions in the attic room here in France. As does the one her granddaughter gives me. The MP and his wives have a leaving party to see me on my way, my favourite meal: curry and rice - and an amazing pink cake.

Photos show the love and affection that came from these lovely women who had done so much to bring a little comfort into our lives. I am grateful to the MP for all the goodwill he had extended to both the project and myself.

I am honoured to meet Senior Chief Nzamane again, and even more honoured to be shown round his garden and given gifts of vegetables for our table. But most of all, I am honoured to hear about his hopes and dreams and plans. His support for Amrita, Ndwali and the project has been unflinching. He has supported and encouraged and spoken honest truth. His generosity in giving the land will be long remembered. I, who have little care for the trappings of royalty, salute him, and wish him well in his endeavours for his people.

Before my last journey within the Eastern Province of Zambia, there is a more official goodbye. With song and dance! Of course! Stage-managed by Ndwali and performed in by Amrita and the Munagra Drama Group. My young friends and Amrita excel themselves in their dancing, the headman from one of the villages gives a rousing speech, and the children enjoy it all enormously.

The best entertainment however is not stage-managed. And it is more than just entertainment. Once again an ethical puzzle rears its head. What do we do about snakes? Amidst the groups arriving for the farewell, a dangerous snake had arrived, in pursuit of a chameleon that had wandered over to the back of our house. Most want to kill the snake and be done with it, but some follow Amrita's lead in making loud sounds to frighten it away. Isaiah rescues the chameleon, but then the snake takes shelter in our bathhouse.

No one will go into the bathhouse after the snake, so Amrita goes into our house. I follow her, guessing what she is up to. There she is. She is donning long socks that reach over her knees going under her long shorts, and a long sleeved jumper that reaches her surgically gloved hands. A large brimmed hat and scarf add to the effect. She goes to check out the bathhouse.

It is empty. The snake had decided that chameleons weren't on the menu that night.

We make a last journey to visit Ndwali's family. The rains are not quite finished with us, and roads are nigh on impassable; several times Ndwali's brothers have to walk in front of the vehicle to ensure our safe passage. They stride through the muddy water, checking out which side is traversable. It is worth it, but it is a bittersweet visit.

There is much joy at seeing my friends and adopted family, and much sadness at knowing this is the last time. It is hard to find the appropriate words to express the feeling of being taken deeply into a family, being made part of it, and being taught so much about family life in a complex culture. I realise that even after five months, I had only just begun to know the basics, and now I have to leave.

It is almost time to go. The goodbyes take many forms. On the last day, many people come to the house; one calls me "shamwa", good friend. I am leaving many good friends in Zambia. I have already said goodbye to one especial friend.

Mrs Nkoma's mother left the previous day, but before leaving she comes right into our house to see me, something she has never done before. Always she would wait outside. But this time she comes in, and sits beside me on the floor, right beside me, close, our bodies touching from hips to toes. Deliberately close, side by side, just as, in a way, we had been side by side with her daughter and son-in-law in their anguish. We do not need words. Her present, lovingly made, sits in our

Leicester home, the small woven ball of leaves and string that preserves the cowpeas leaves against hunger to come.

The last goodbye is especially deeply felt. We have become sisters. In our daily meetings over the last few months I have seen Mrs Nkoma grow from being a woman spinning round in the depths of despair into a strong and determined matriarch.

On this final day we sit shelling beans in the sun, enjoying each other's company. I have just returned from town and am feeling rather puzzled by people's reactions to me in the shops. I don't have a second head, or a wart growing on my nose, or anything else very strange, so why did they look at me as if....then it sinks in. I was in town, they do not know me, and here in the villages they know me. I had forgotten - that I am white! They were treating me as a white woman.

Mrs Nkoma's delighted laughter rings in my ears. It is quite a joke. We have both forgotten I am foreign.

I see her now, striding out, I see her strength and courage, and it gives me courage too, and a sense of purpose to help others go beyond the barriers of culture and race to truly know each other, and befriend each other. Her friendship is here with me now, as I write.

They are all with me, and of course Amrita, Ndwali, Gotami, Esther and Naomi who travelled with me on to Lusaka. There in the airport I cried as I left my family in Zambia with whom I had shared my life, my faith and much irreverent laughter in the last six months. I see them waving as the plane taxies down the runway and lifts me high above them into the skies and away.

My life changed by my being with these friends. The process that began shortly after my fortieth birthday still gathers momentum. The last words written in my journal as the plane swept me away, are these:

"I recognise my being here in a new way, I know now why I never wanted to go to Africa or India or any country with such suffering. I never wanted to see the pain of others lives, let alone feel it. Yet here I am. I was avoiding my destiny for so long, and I know why. To feel this pain, our pain is like having a raw open wound within, that oh so often has salt put in it. Inner tears, a lake of sorrow. And not just for these people here. Even here the plight of Kosovo echoes, and my old call to the former Yugoslavia returns...There is suffering of sorts in every corner of this world of ours. And I am called to it all.

The bodhisattva vow is very live for me in this moment. Time to come home for a little while, to share, to learn, to teach, to heal a little, and then go on, to wherever there is greatest need. No matter what this "I" wants, and no matter what this "I" fears...

What are my important learnings? Brother Helmont, founder of a project, which is a role model for Tithandizane, had it in a nutshell "for three months keep your mouth shut and your eyes open".

And yet we have to talk too, just a little, answering questions honestly and openly, and asking the relevant ones too; and in the midst of it all to somehow find some calm and peace within. To learn patience, then we can follow where our paths lead, where the demands are, the people's needs. And to be always like a beginner, ready to learn from anyone, at any time, and show it too. To speak sparingly but love generously, to suspend judgement, and hear what is not being said. And just be with each person we meet, with each situation, and just do what is necessary at any given time."

POSTSCRIPT

I wake up early this morning, in our retreat centre in France. I am here, but my heart is back with my friends in Zambia. Here in this quiet corner of the French countryside, the Amida community helps people rest and be replenished from their often demanding lives. We also offer a place to train. Buddhist training that helps equip us to go wherever there is need.

I bring back what I learned in Zambia. I have learnt about a different way of living in a culture that is probably more civil than any I have previously known. - A culture where the many rules and customs protect the feeling of community that we have almost lost in the West. A culture where love of song and rhythm permeates lives, alongside a deep spirituality. I cried when I had to leave there. I did not want to go. I made many friends, grew to love the country and learnt so much.

Together we learnt, and above all I learnt that friendship is the biggest part of this story. The Buddha said to Ananda, one of his disciples, "friendship is the whole of life". I heartily agree.

In Zambia I found friendship that crossed the

frontiers of race, culture, colour, class and gender. The name of the project is Tithandizane. "Tithandizane" means "we help each other". I helped as much as I could. More than anything I found myself helped time and time again. It was a precious experience.

Zambia is a land of peace and great joy, in some respects a Pure Land. In the bush villages a sense of community and openhearted friendship still exists. I hope this book will spread greater understanding of Zambia and how life can be in other cultures.

I hope it may encourage others to go forth in whatever ways they are called to do, whether it is in foreign climes or on their own back doorstep. Seeing the pain in Zambia made me only too aware, not just of the problems that face the people and their children there, but also those that face our children growing up in the West.

A LITTLE MORE ABOUT ZAMBIA

In Zambia seventy-two different tribes co-exist peaceably; it is a country that offers a peaceful haven amidst many other countries torn apart by internal strife. This is also a culture where community comes before the individual. Steve Biko, who came from South Africa, expressed it beautifully:

".... *In the traditional African culture there is no such thing as two friends...all commonly shared their secrets, joys and woes. No one felt unnecessarily an intruder into someone else's business. The curiosity manifested was welcome. It came out of a desire to share. This pattern one would find in all age groups. House visiting was always a feature of the elderly folk's way of life. No reason was needed as a basis for visits. It was all part of our deep concern for each other.*"

However, they now live this way amidst extremes of suffering. Some figures suggest 31% of the people are infected with HIV in Zambia. A report from Michael Kelly in One World Africa, November 2000 estimated that in Zambia one third of children under fifteen are orphans, having lost one or both parents. Chisenga Kabuse of the Pan African news agency wrote in

October 2000 that more than one million Zambians are expected to die of AIDS and that life expectancy had dropped to thirty-eight years. The world AIDS conference in Madrid estimated that within five years the life expectancy will be down to twenty-nine.

I can bear witness to the truth of those figures. Indeed I fear that they are a grave under-estimation. I saw villages that already seemed to consist mostly of children and old people. I saw children missing school in order to attempt to grow enough food for their families.

This is not all. Zambia's problems predated the onset of AIDS. Malaria is endemic, measles is still a killer, many suffer the after-effects of polio. Tuberculosis is rife. Water-borne diseases are common in villages where often even the well water is unsafe. Malnutrition adds to the problems, crops grow poorly in soil that is little more than sand, and many of the crops have been introduced unwisely, depleting the soil even further. Fewer than half the babies born survive to adulthood.

Recently I returned to Zambia. Sadly it was to conduct Amrita's funeral. Malaria had claimed another victim. But she lives on in the project she founded that now grows and thrives in the hands of the local people.

ABOUT MODGALA

Sister Modgala is a founder member of the Amida Trust. Her growing understanding of the spiritual life and the need for spiritual care led her to become a nun in 1998.

She has a background in psychology and mental health and a particular interest in social activism and applied Buddhist psychology.

She has travelled on behalf of Amida to Zambia, France, Vietnam and Sarajevo.

In India she founded the Amida Delhi project.

Currently she is based at the Amida London Centre where she offers teachings, retreats and support in the local community.

Amida London: www.amidalondon.org.uk

ABOUT AMIDA TRUST

Amida Trust is a charity (non-profit organisation) registered in the UK that provides the legal sponsorship for the activities of the Amida community. The charity is a trust and has a board of trustees who oversee its operations.

The Amida Order came into being in the summer of 1998 when three people took bodhisattva vows with Dharmavidya. Initially the intention was not so much to create a new sangha as to allow those who wished to do so to affirm their commitment to full time Buddhist training in a socially engaged context. Over the intervening years the sangha has developed and the Order has clarified its orientation and structure.

The Amida Order is involved in religious work: teaching Pureland Buddhist Dharma, psychological work: the trust provides professional training for psychotherapists, and socially & culturally engaged projects all over the world.

www.amidatrust.com

www.buddhistpsychology.com